THE EASY HABITS JOURNAL

Better Habits in 12 Weeks

DR. HAYDEN FINCH

Copyright © 2025 by Callisto Publishing LLC
Cover and internal design © 2025 by Callisto Publishing LLC
Illustrations © mxsbmbrg/Shutterstock
Art Director: Amanda Kirk and Lisa Schreiber
Art Producers: Samantha Ulban and Stacey Stambaugh
Editors: Emily Angell and Adrian Potts
Production Editor: Ruth Sakata Corley and Rachel Taenzler
Production Manager: Martin Worthington

Callisto Publishing and the colophon are registered trademarks of Callisto Publishing LLC.

All rights reserved. No part of this book may be reproduced in any form or by any electronic or mechanical means including information storage and retrieval systems—except in the case of brief quotations embodied in critical articles or reviews—without permission in writing from its publisher, Sourcebooks LLC.

Published by Callisto Publishing LLC C/O Sourcebooks LLC
P.O. Box 4410, Naperville, Illinois 60567-4410
(630) 961-3900
callistopublishing.com

Originally published as *Habits: A 12-Week Journal to Change Your Habits, Track Your Progress, and Achieve Your Goals* in 2021 in the United States of America by Callisto, an imprint of Callisto Publishing LLC. This edition issued based on the paperback edition published in 2021 in the United States of America by Callisto, an imprint of Callisto Publishing LLC.

Printed and bound in the United States of America.
VP 10 9 8 7 6 5 4 3 2 1

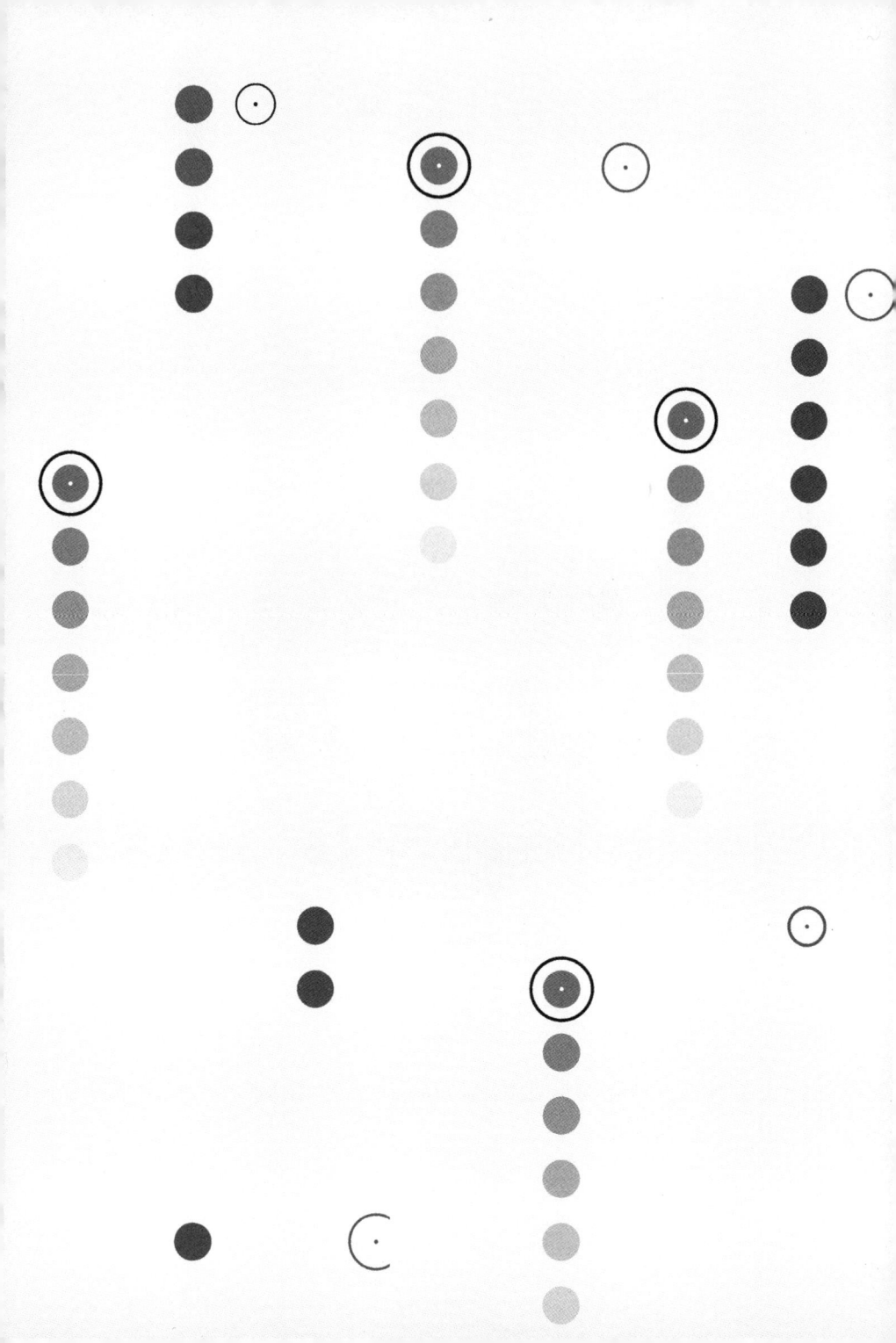

"Motivation is what gets you started. Habit is what keeps you going."

—JIM RYUN

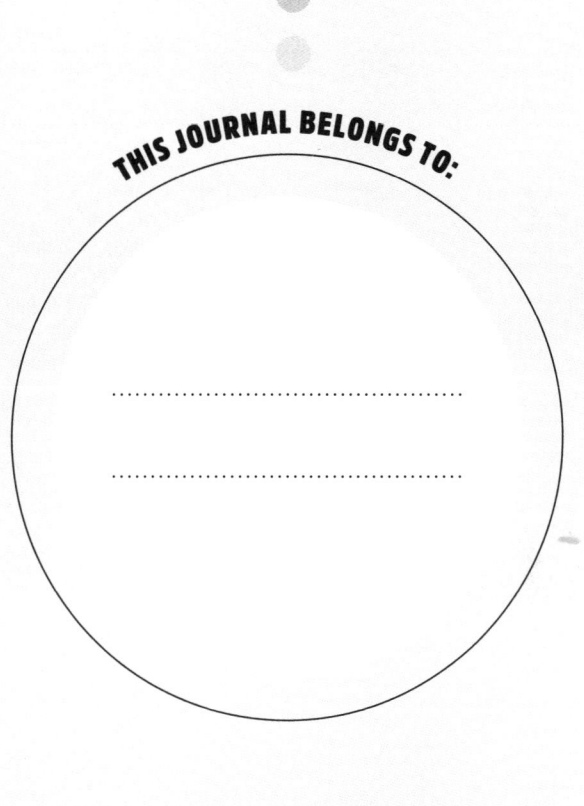

THIS JOURNAL BELONGS TO:

....

....

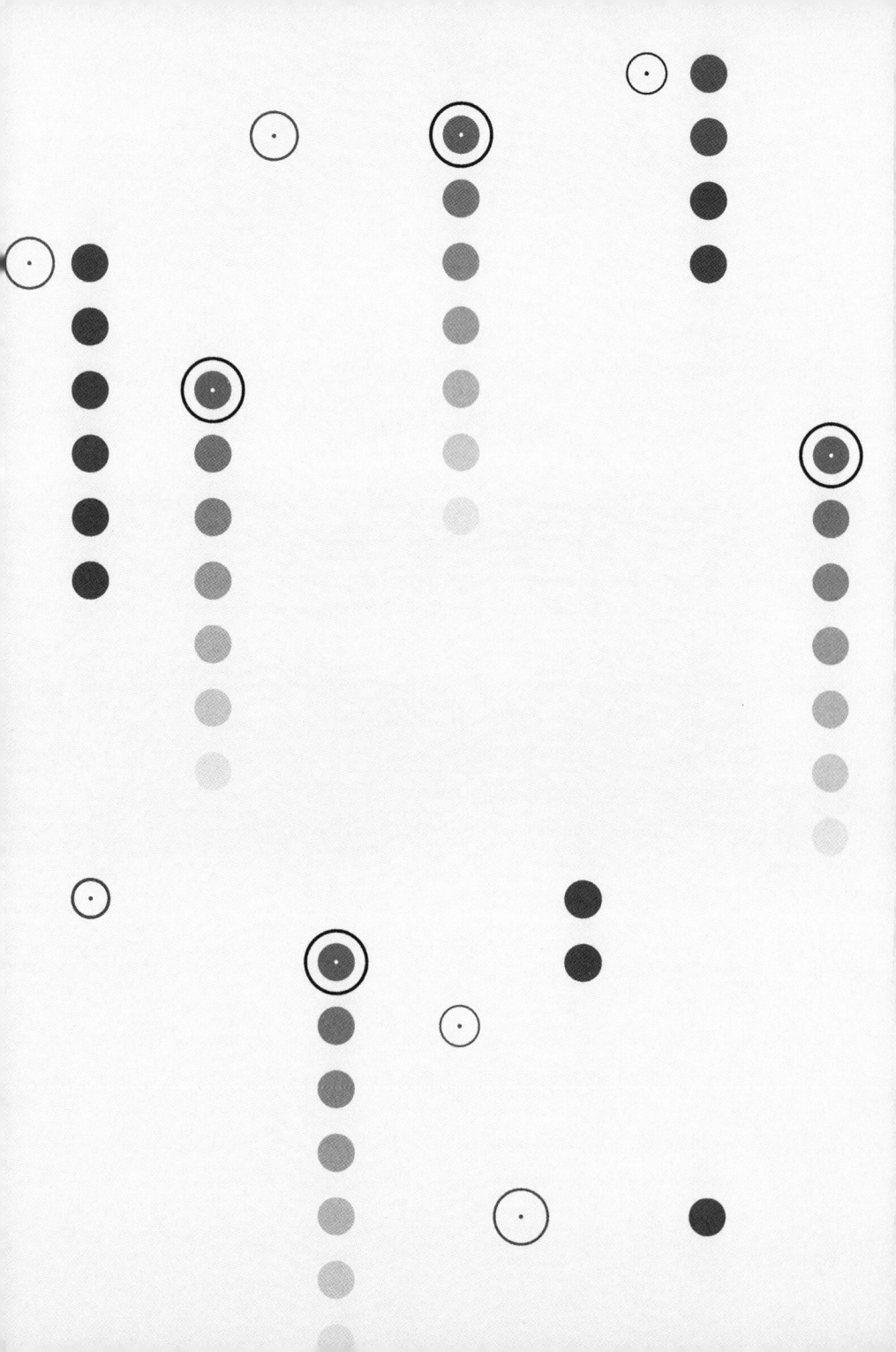

Contents

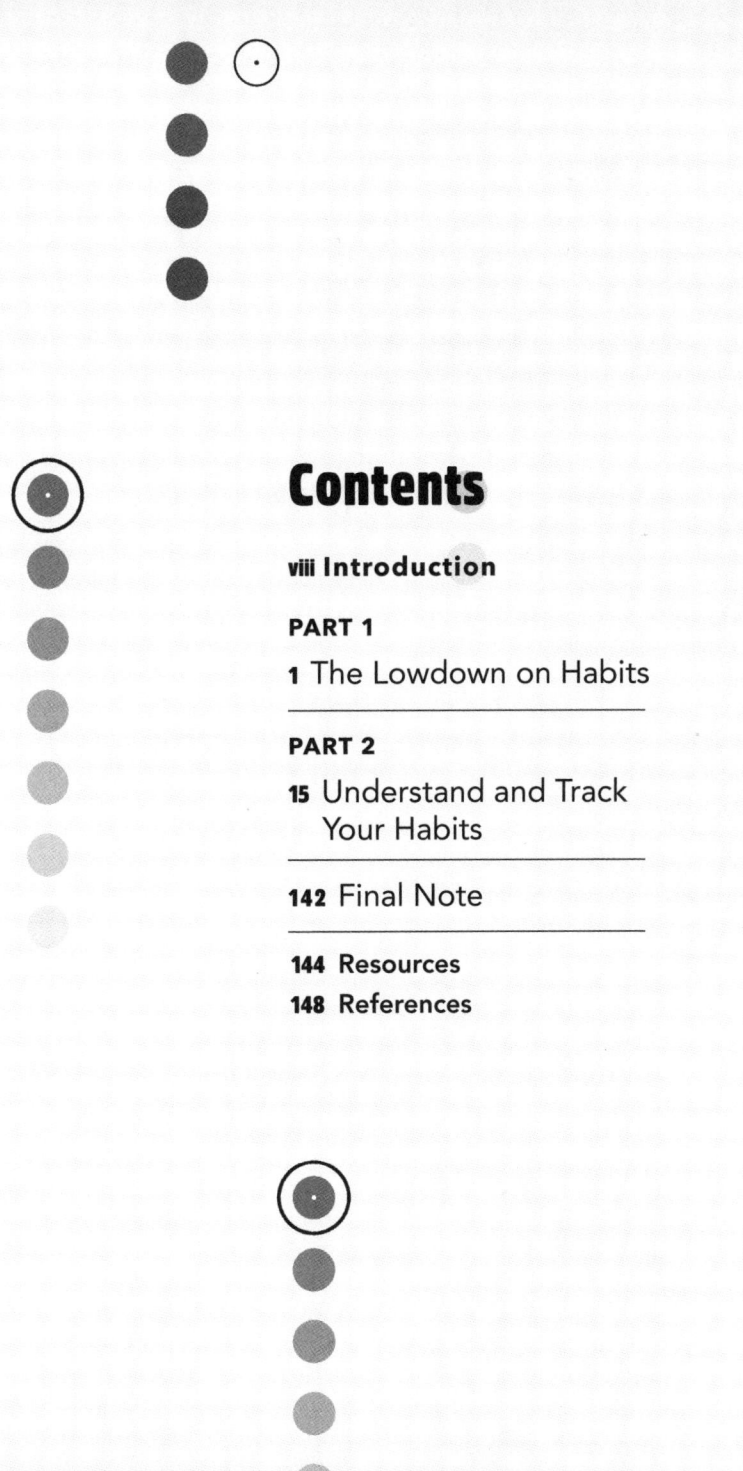

viii Introduction

PART 1
1 The Lowdown on Habits

PART 2
15 Understand and Track Your Habits

142 Final Note

144 Resources
148 References

Introduction

If you're like any other human on this planet, you've probably picked up a handful of bad habits over the years. You've also probably tried to kick those habits more than once, with limited success. Or maybe you've tried to add a healthy habit to your lifestyle and found yourself struggling to make it stick. Somehow, bad habits are easy to establish and hard to break, while, frustratingly, healthy habits are difficult to establish and easy to drop.

But just because it's hard to change your habits doesn't mean it's impossible. Psychology has shown us that habits have specific components, and our ability to change our behavior improves dramatically when we thoroughly address each of those individual components. That's where this simple-to-use journal comes in. This journal will make it easy to tackle your habits from every angle, using important insights from the science of habits, practical tips, encouraging quotes, positive affirmations, writing prompts to help you examine your habits more thoroughly, and all the tracking tools you need to stay on course. No matter what kind of habit you have, by completing this journal, you'll be well on your way to changing it.

Before we get too far along, I should introduce myself. My name is Dr. Hayden Finch, and I'm a licensed clinical psychologist who specializes in helping people change their behavior. Over the past 15 years, I've studied psychology and human behavior and learned a lot about how our behaviors (and especially our habits) influence our success, our goals, and the way we feel about ourselves and our lives. All the clients I've treated have struggled with habits they wanted to change, from procrastination and people-pleasing to tardiness and overeating. Together, we used research-backed strategies to change these habits and keep them on the right track.

My therapy clients often experience anxiety or sadness, or feel overwhelmed as they change their habits, and you may, too. These negative feelings often come up when we're dealing with unhealthy habits—they're frequently the reason we establish these habits in the first place and why it can be so hard to change them. These feelings are a normal part of the process.

Keep in mind, though, that if your feelings of sadness or anxiety feel unmanageable, you should consult a licensed mental health professional for individualized care.

In treating my own clients, I've learned that overcoming bad habits isn't simply a matter of motivation. It's much deeper than that. But no matter what behavior you're trying to change, simply keeping track of it can play a major role in changing it. And if you supplement that monitoring with deep critical thinking about the habit, and then develop a specific plan for addressing the unique components of habits, you'll be well on your way to finally making lasting change. That's why I wrote this habit journal—to give you a dedicated space to monitor your behavior, keep yourself on track, and guide yourself through the questions you need to answer on the path to better habits. The first step to letting your brain rewire itself and moving toward your goals is picking up this journal.

PART 1
THE LOWDOWN ON HABITS

"We are what we repeatedly do.
Excellence, then, is not an act, but a habit."

– WILLIAM DURANT

A common mistake people make when trying to change their behavior is skipping straight to the "change" part. But that's like a football team just walking onto the field without any idea of who their opponent is. That's not a great idea. Before a game, a team usually tries to learn about their opponent's strengths and weaknesses as well as their own strengths and weaknesses, how previous teams have defeated their opponent, and the conditions on the field. It's the same with changing habits: Before you change anything, it's important to understand what you're dealing with.

Part 1 is all about that preparation. In this section, you'll learn what exactly a habit is, how habits are formed, and how to make good habits stick. This foundation will prepare you for the changes you want to make in part 2.

WHAT ARE HABITS?

Whenever you repeatedly engage in a certain behavior when in a certain situation, your brain takes notice and will start to automate the process. It says, "Hey, I noticed you've started hitting the snooze button twice when your alarm goes off. You probably want to keep doing that, so I'll go ahead and automate that for you so you won't even have to think about it anymore." Your brain then remembers that this situation should lead to this behavior, and that's how you develop a habit—good or bad.

Habits are automatic responses our brains create when they are triggered by specific cues—other people, our thoughts or feelings, another behavior, or things in the environment. Once you notice one of those cues (e.g., seeing a social media app on your phone's home screen), your brain immediately triggers your default behavior (opening the app and beginning to scroll). Habits tend to be fast and efficient, and they take very little thought, which helps them stick.

A VERY BRIEF HISTORY OF THE SCIENCE OF HABITS

Psychologists began studying habits in the late 1800s, when William James, one of the "founding fathers" of psychology, wrote a series of essays on habits. In those essays, he argued that our brains learn from experience and that habits are formed by two things: (1) circumstances that promote the behavior, and (2) consistently and repeatedly performing the behavior until it becomes a habit. His initial ideas were refined over the next century, but they remain influential in our basic understanding of the science of habits.

In the first half of the 20th century, habit research focused heavily on how animals learn. In the 1940s, B. F. Skinner used that research to develop his theory that we're more likely to repeat behaviors that are rewarded and less likely to repeat behaviors that are punished. In the 1950s and 1960s, psychological researchers began to investigate the extent to which thoughts, choices, and motivations contribute to behavior and habit. Research investigating how habit formation is influenced by environmental and psychological factors continued through the remainder of the 20th century.

The 21st century saw an explosion in research on the neuroscience of habits. Now, we understand that habits are complex psychological phenomena, far more sophisticated than simply performing a chosen behavior; they're influenced by rewards, punishments, thoughts, motivations, and basic neuroscience (Graybiel, 2008).

THE STEPS OF HABIT FORMATION: CUE-BEHAVIOR-REWARD

From the science of habits, we've learned that they are formed through what is essentially a three-step process: trigger, then behavior, then reward (Wood & Rünger, 2016). Let's break that down.

First, there's a trigger, or cue. The cue can be something obvious (like an alarm or the smell of a particular food) or something subtle (like entering a certain room or sitting in a particular way). It can be triggered by outside stimuli (like hearing someone make a comment about you or experiencing a particular event). It can also be triggered by internal stimuli (like a thought, memory, emotion, or physical sensation).

Then the cue triggers a behavior. The behavior can be something you actively *do* (like stopping for coffee or hitting the "Next Episode" button again), or it can be something you *don't* do (like going to the gym or adding vegetables to your plate).

Finally, there's a reward. Like cues, rewards can be obvious (like fitting into a desired clothing size) or subtle (like feeling increased self-esteem or a more positive outlook). They can also be both internal (relief from uncomfortable emotions, escape from bothersome thoughts) or external (praise from a boss, encouragement from friends).

Here's how it plays out: Feeling groggy when you wake up (cue) triggers the urge to hit the snooze button (behavior), which allows you to sleep more and delay starting your day (reward). Or seeing a T-shirt from your local gym reminds you that exercise helps you feel more energetic (cue), which encourages you to exercise (behavior), leaving you with more energy and a feeling of accomplishment (reward). Or a notification on your calendar (cue) reminds you to schedule lunch with your coworkers (behavior), which is rewarded with laughter, a brain break, and delicious food (reward). Almost all habits fit this model if you dig deep enough to discover the cues and rewards. (They can be hidden!)

HABITS IMPACT OUR MENTAL, EMOTIONAL, PHYSICAL, AND SPIRITUAL SELF

Because so many of our behaviors become habitual, our overall well-being is deeply connected to our daily habits. Affirmatively engaging in healthy habits has an impact on how we function mentally, emotionally, physically, and spiritually. These habits may strengthen our memory or attention span, increase our energy level or emotional stability, or make us feel connected to a greater purpose. Many habits may even impact us in several ways at once. For instance, if you take up an exercise habit because you want to become physically stronger, you may also get the added benefits of lowered anxiety and depression, clearer thoughts, and time for quiet contemplation.

Similarly, when we affirmatively engage in unhealthy habits or habitually neglect to engage in healthy behaviors, our well-being suffers—again, often in several different ways at once. That's why the habits you choose become a critical part of your overall wellness.

THE DIFFERENCE BETWEEN GOOD HABITS AND BAD HABITS

We all have bad habits. It's part of being alive and doing our best to get through every day. Most of us skip the floss once in a while, stay up too late, procrastinate, or don't get five servings of fruits and veggies every day. That's normal. And even when you have a life that's objectively good, you almost definitely still experience stress, which makes you more susceptible to temptation and bad habits.

The difference between good habits and bad habits is in whether they support your values and long-term goals. When you are clear on what you value and what your goals are, your habits determine your success in aligning your life with those values and reaching those goals. Part 2 will help you clarify your values and goals so you can establish habits accordingly.

Good habits are behaviors that are consistent with your values or help you move closer to achieving your goals. By contrast, bad habits are behaviors that don't contribute to achieving your long-term goals or, even worse, distract or detract from achieving those goals. For example, maybe you value health and physical fitness, and your long-term goal is to develop the endurance to go on a hike with your family. A good habit might be to pack your gym clothes for tomorrow, whereas a bad habit might be to use your phone late in the evening (which makes it hard for you to sleep, leaving you tired in the morning and discouraging your pre-work exercise routine). Or maybe you value financial independence and security, and your long-term goal is to pay off all your credit card debt. A good habit might be to save 10 percent of each paycheck, whereas a bad habit might be to ignore your budget and spend impulsively.

THE BENEFITS OF GOOD HABITS

Not only do good habits help you establish a life that's aligned with your values, they have lots of other benefits, too.

You're more likely to maintain the results of your goal if you achieved that goal by developing good habits as opposed to achieving it through a short period of concerted effort. So, if your goal is a decluttered home, you're more likely to maintain it if you got there through developing the habit of discarding two items every time you buy one new item rather than if you got there by decluttering your whole house over a long weekend. An annual weekend-long declutter-fest could be a helpful behavior, but it's not a habit, so your likelihood of being consistent with it is lower.

Plus, once we see that our habits are producing *results*, our motivation to keep going increases. When you can see that your habit of doing some light stretches each morning reduces your pain, you're much more motivated to keep that habit going.

Habits also provide structure to our lives. Many of our habits are time-based, meaning that we do them at a particular time of day or as part of a routine. Structure is helpful for keeping us focused on what's really important to us. Without it, we tend to get distracted and end up dedicating our time to activities that aren't actually meaningful to us, like TV or social media, just by default.

GOOD HABITS CAN HELP WITH EVERY PART OF LIFE

Small changes in our daily routines can produce massive changes throughout our lives, improving our overall well-being. For example, improving your mental health by making a habit of journaling each day can help you improve other areas of your life, too. Not only will you feel better emotionally, which was the initial goal, but you'll likely also see that your relationships improve, you're able to fight off illnesses faster, and you are more productive. This is true for all good habits: When you can firmly establish a few healthy behaviors as habitual, you're likely to see improvements far beyond your intended results. These may extend to your relationships, cognitive functioning, work or school performance, finances, sleep, stress level, emotional well-being, diet, exercise, physical health, creativity, productivity, and spiritual health.

HOW DO YOU MAKE GOOD HABITS STICK?

Making good habits stick requires two steps.

STEP 1: Stop automatically triggering the unwanted habit.

This requires that you determine what cues trigger the habit and then restructure the environment to limit how often the unwanted habit is triggered. For example, if you want to quit biting your nails, step 1 is to determine that bringing your hand near your face triggers the nail-biting, and then come up with activities to keep your hands away from your face. As habits become stronger, our brains consider fewer responses in a given situation and simply repeat the habitual response. That's why stopping the old habit also involves training yourself to begin making new responses to these cues (like catching yourself with your hands near your face and immediately choosing an alternative position).

STEP 2: Establish the new habit.
This requires that you start a new behavior and repeat it in similar situations until it becomes automatized. To quit biting your nails, you might want to start taking out a knitting project or a fidget toy whenever you watch TV to keep your hands busy. When you can take these steps, your good habits will begin to stick.

WHY YOU SHOULD KEEP A HABIT JOURNAL

Unfortunately, your desire to change a habit won't necessarily be enough to produce results. Changing habits doesn't come down to willpower; it comes down to knowing the psychology behind habits and using it to your advantage. That's where this journal fits in. There is a strong research base showing that monitoring your behavior, with a habit journal or similar tool, is a powerful resource in actually making lasting change (Patel, Brooks, & Bennett, 2019). Tracking your behavior allows you to monitor your progress, identify cues triggering the behavior you want to change, and detect areas interfering with your success. Understanding these factors is the best way to make lasting change.

WHY 12 WEEKS?

Exactly how long it takes to establish new habits has long been a matter of debate. You might have read that it takes 21 or 30 or some other number of days, but research shows it usually takes longer than that for most habits to stick.

Although there are many factors that influence how long it takes to establish any given habit, this journal uses a 12-week time frame for several reasons. Firstly, 12 weeks gives you plenty of time to identify what you want to change, track your progress, and recalibrate your goals if needed. Secondly, committing to 12 weeks gives you a clear and manageable amount of time to focus your efforts. Finally, by focusing on the behaviors you want to establish over a 12-week period, those behaviors should begin to occur with less thought and eventually become automatic—which is to say, a habit!

Once you have a solid foundation in place, you can use the tools you've learned with this journal to consolidate good habits well into the future.

HOW TO USE THIS BOOK

You can use this book to keep track of old habits you want to break or new habits you want to develop. Monitoring your habits as you work to make changes will help you stay consistent and maintain positive results. You can start by establishing a goal you want to work toward. Then use the questions and prompts in this journal to determine what healthy habits will move you toward that goal and what unhealthy habits are getting in your way. You can use the evidence-based tips in this journal to solidify your new healthy habit, complete the journal prompts to dive deeper into the psychology behind your old, unhealthy habit, and use the positive affirmations to keep yourself motivated and on track.

The daily, weekly, and 28-day check-ins will help keep you on track and give you a place to record observations, evaluate what's going well, adjust for any struggles, and monitor your progress. On the 28-day check-in pages, there is space to track three different habits. Feel free to track fewer habits for a more focused approach or duplicate the template on your own if you're tracking more than three habits. Finally, reap the rewards of all your effort by firmly establishing your new habit.

FAQ

Even though you're highly motivated to change your habits and ready to get started, you might have some questions about how to actually make this work for you. If those questions go unanswered, they could lead to self-doubt and hold you back. With that in mind, here are answers to some of the most frequently asked questions about starting new habits.

Can I pick up more than one new habit at a time?
You absolutely can change more than one habit at a time, but remember to keep it as simple as possible. The more you try to change about yourself at once, the more challenging it will be for your brain to adapt to all the changes. You may want to consider starting with one habit and then add a second once you feel like the first is firmly established.

How do I commit to my new habits if I'm traveling or not on my normal routine?
Travel, vacation, or other disruptions to our daily lives definitely make it difficult to stick to new habits. But you can keep your momentum alive by establishing a backup plan ahead of time. For example, if the habit you're trying to establish is going to the gym three or four times each week, develop a plan to stick to the habit while traveling by substituting a 30-minute walk or a no-equipment exercise routine on YouTube.

What if I forget to check in with my habit journal?
Simple forgetfulness is one of the most common issues people run into with keeping a habit journal. In fact, missing an entry can lead some people to just abandon the journal altogether. They tell themselves that if the journal is incomplete or imperfect, it's

useless, or that once the habit is broken, it's hard to start again. If you have these thoughts, be compassionate with yourself. Remind yourself that you're still making progress, even if it's not perfect, and that some data about your habit is much more helpful than none.

What do I do if I don't have time to write in a journal every day?
Even if your goal is just to establish a new habit of washing the dishes as soon as you're done eating, you're actually picking up *two* new habits: washing the dishes *and* using your habit journal. In part 2, you'll learn tips and strategies for establishing new habits and overcoming roadblocks. The same roadblocks and helpful tips that apply to establishing your new habits also apply to using this journal, so use those strategies if you're finding you don't have time for your journal. It's common for people to think that keeping track of their behavior is "too much effort," "too time-consuming," or "too tedious," and these beliefs can be barriers to success. Remember that you don't have to fill out your journal completely every single day; if you only have a moment to just briefly check in on the basics, do that and skip the rest. It's okay to skip a day of recording every once in a while. But if you're finding that you're away from your journal for multiple consecutive days, remind yourself why you started this journal in the first place, review your values and goals, and reread the section "Why You Should Keep a Habit Journal" (page 8).

What should I do if I start slipping with my habit?
Another common reason people abandon their habit journals is because they are embarrassed to admit in writing that they haven't been consistent with their habit. It can definitely feel demoralizing to document the days or weeks when you're slipping, but remind yourself that you're still gathering useful

information by documenting the obstacles you encountered that interfered with your success on those days. See those lapses and slips as learning opportunities instead of failures.

What do I do when I want to give up?
Go ahead and prepare yourself: There *will* be days when you want to give up and just go back to your old behaviors. That's perfectly normal. When this happens to you, review your values and goals from part 2 to remind yourself why you started on this journey in the first place. Take a few days to regroup if needed, and then refocus on why this habit matters to you.

YOU'RE READY TO START

Now that you understand what habits are, the psychology behind them, how they're formed, how they impact your life, and what keeps them going, you've established the foundation you need to start changing them. In part 2, you'll discover how to set goals and choose which habits you want to ditch, change, or improve. You'll also work through a series of journal exercises to dive deeper into the behaviors you want to change. Once you specify exactly what you want to work on, you'll be ready to actually start changing your behavior, and part 2 will equip you with the evidence-based tips and strategies you need for success.

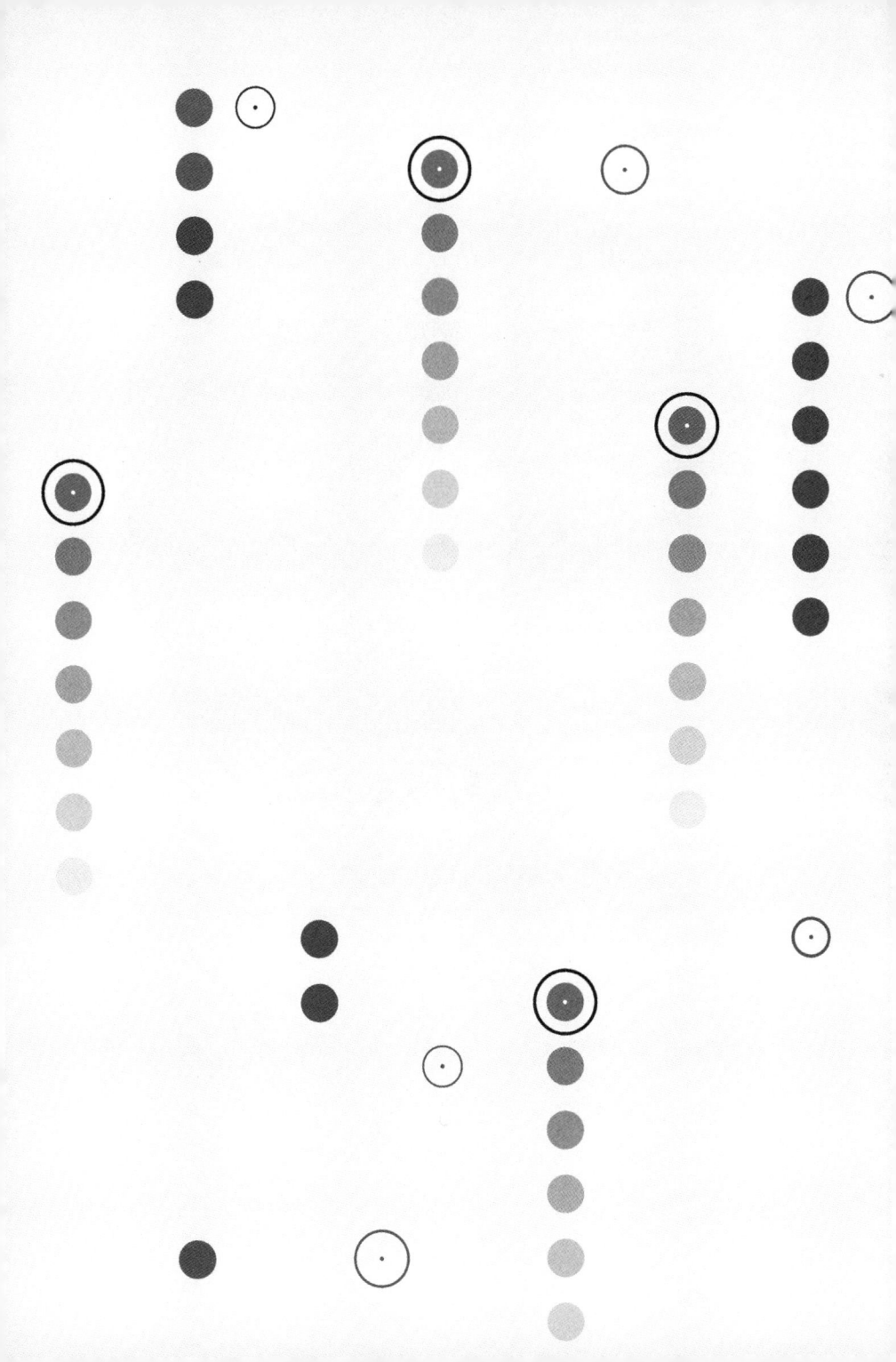

PART 2

UNDERSTAND AND TRACK YOUR HABITS

"Goal + Toll = SUCCESS. Establish your goal. Be prepared to pay the price in terms of time, money, energy and credit-sharing, and you'll succeed. Remember: Triumph is made up of two words: TRY and UMPH."

—ROBERT SCHULLER

In part 1, you learned about the psychology of cues and rewards and how they keep habits going. Now, it's time to put that knowledge into practice by actually changing your behavior. In part 2, you'll specify exactly what you want to change, establish a plan for making that change, and prepare yourself for some common obstacles in changing habits. I'll also give you a heads-up on some of the most common mistakes people make when they're trying to establish new habits so you won't have to repeat those mistakes.

GET ALIGNED WITH YOUR VALUES TO BETTER UNDERSTAND YOUR GOALS AND HABITS

Your values are the guiding principles for your life; they reflect what is most important to you. Ideally, the way you spend your time mirrors your values. Unfortunately, sometimes our behaviors stray from our values. Here's an example: Most of us value our grandmothers more than television. But given the choice between calling Grandma and watching Netflix, we often end up waist-deep in an *Orange Is the New Black* binge with the call to Grandma pushed off to another day. Sometimes, living this way can feel pleasurable or easier in the short term. But when our lives are aligned with our values, we tend to feel more positively about our lives and feel more centered overall.

Before you decide what habits you want to target with this journal, let's make sure you're clear on what your values are. This isn't a quiz to see if you can guess what the "right" or "best" values are; there's no right or wrong way to structure your values. Instead, try to consider what *you* value, not what your family or society *wants* you to value.

Reflect on these questions: What do you think is your main purpose in life? What do you want to be remembered for?

....
....
....
....
....

Next, rank the importance of each of the following areas from 1 (most important) to 10 (least important). You likely value most or all of these areas, and it can be hard to rank them, but challenging yourself to make tough choices between your values can be enlightening.

- [ ] FAMILY RELATIONSHIPS
- [ ] FRIENDSHIPS
- [ ] ROMANTIC RELATIONSHIPS
- [ ] WORK/CAREER
- [ ] EDUCATION
- [ ] PERSONAL GROWTH AND DEVELOPMENT
- [ ] RECREATION OR LEISURE
- [ ] SPIRITUALITY OR RELIGION
- [ ] HELPING YOUR COMMUNITY
- [ ] HEALTH

Now, combine what you learned from these two exercises to determine what you value most.

....
....
....
....
....

WHAT GOALS DO YOU WANT TO SET FOR YOURSELF?

Now that you know your values, the next step in changing your habits is to establish what your goals are. Values determine how you want to live your life, and goals are the behaviors that help you turn that vision into a reality. For example, if you realize that your values involve focusing on personal growth, you might choose behaviors that help you learn concrete strategies to increase self-confidence.

Review your values and consider what achievements could help you live a life more aligned with those values. Some useful goals might be to: get your own apartment, purchase a car, develop a healthy romantic relationship, make a good friend, keep current on your bills, complete your education, find an enriching job, stay true to your religious faith, socialize with friends or family, have a peaceful mind, have fun, be physically fit, sleep well and wake refreshed, be comfortable in your own body, keep control of your temper, and so on. Make sure the goal is something *you* want. It's great to be inspired by others, but the goal needs to be important to you.

What do *you* want to accomplish?

....

....

....

....

....

WHAT HABITS DO YOU WANT TO DITCH, CHANGE, OR IMPROVE?

Your habits are the daily actions that either help you reach your goals or interfere with your goals. So, if your goal is to learn concrete strategies to increase self-confidence, a habit that might support that goal is reading a bit each day about how to improve your self-confidence. A habit that might interfere with that goal is gaming for so many hours each day that you don't have any free time to learn confidence-boosting strategies.

As you consider the habits you want to ditch, change, or improve, begin by looking at which habits you'd like to integrate into your everyday life and which habits you'd like to eliminate.

Considering your goals and your values, which of your current habits is keeping you from reaching your goals?

....
....
....
....
....

What new healthy habits would help you reach your goals?

....
....
....
....
....

START SMALL

Now that you've identified how you want to change, it's time to figure out where to start. For some, this can be one of the most challenging parts of establishing a new habit.

One of the greatest mistakes people make when starting a new habit is capitalizing on their motivation and excitement by making massive changes right away. This is a common reason why New Year's resolutions fail—we go hard right out of the gate with a complete overhaul, working at an unsustainable pace, and then our progress falls apart just a few weeks later.

If you want lasting success with your habit, it's important to start small—*way* smaller than you're thinking. Think about it like this: Pilots need to only make tiny micro-adjustments to the speed and direction of a plane to land safely in their destination. If their adjustments are too big, they end up way off course.

It's the same when establishing habits. When you make massive changes to your life to accommodate a new habit, it throws everything else in your life off. Suddenly, you're spending an hour at the gym five days a week, which means you lost five hours that you would have otherwise spent doing other activities. Most of us don't account for that when we commit to these habits, and we lose our consistency when we realize that we're dropping balls because we're trying to keep this habit going.

Instead, make micro-adjustments. Start where you are and make the tiniest possible change. Allow your brain, body, and life to adjust to this change. And then make the next tiniest possible change. Let's say the habit you're trying to establish is to write down three things you're grateful for every night. Determine where you're currently at, and then adjust that by the smallest amount possible. If you're currently not gratitude journaling at all, jumping all the way to a daily practice is a massive change—it might not seem like it, but it really is. Instead, try setting a goal to write down three things you're grateful for *once* this week. If you're successful, try to repeat it or increase it by just a smidge next week (like maybe *twice* that week). If you're not successful, this shows you just how difficult it is to fit this habit into your life. Examine what got in the way, adjust for those factors, and either try the same goal again or adjust downward to be even easier (like maybe writing down *one* thing you're grateful for each night).

How often are you currently performing your desired behavior?

....

....

What is the smallest possible change you could make?

....

....

This method will feel like a slow way to get to the finish line, but think about it like the fable of the tortoise and the hare: Slow and steady wins the race. You can go hard at first, try to force the habit into your life, and probably end up completely off track a few weeks later. Or you can ease into it, adjust your life around the new habit, and actually build consistency and stability.

DEFINE YOUR HABIT

Now that you've decided on a habit to change and identified how to start small, it's time to tweak that habit a bit. To have the best shot at success, our behaviors need to meet five criteria summarized by the acronym **SMART**.

First, your habit needs to be **Specific**: What *exactly* do you want to do? "Read" is vague—does reading the Facebook newsfeed count? But "Read a book" is more specific.

Next, your habit needs to be **Measurable**, meaning it needs a number attached to it so you'll know for sure whether you did it. "Read for 15 minutes a day" is measurable because you can count and determine whether that was accomplished. You can measure your habit in terms of how long (engage in 10 minutes of meditation), how much (drink 60 ounces of water), or how many (perform three kind deeds). Also, keep in mind that some habits might be measured in "streaks" (floss *three days in a row*) or frequency (floss *three times per week*).

Your habit also needs to be **Attainable**, meaning it's the tiniest bit more challenging than what you're currently doing. "Read for an hour every day" isn't attainable if you're currently not reading at all, but "Read for 15 minutes three times a week" might be.

Next, your habit should be personally **Relevant**, meaning that it's important to *you*, not just your family, your friends, or society. For example, maybe reading is important to you because it contributes to your goal of increasing self-confidence and honors your value of making time for personal growth.

Finally, your habit should be **Time-Limited**, meaning there's a deadline by which you hope to firmly establish the habit. This book makes it easy by providing you with a 12-week time frame so you can approach your goals in a steady and sustainable way and keep yourself accountable over a fixed period of time.

When you combine all five parts, this complete SMART habit would be: "Establish a habit to read a book (S) for 15 minutes (M), three times a week (A), over the next 12 weeks (T) so I can feel more confident and honor my value of making time for personal growth (R)."

Now, tweak your own habit with the SMART criteria:

S ....
....
....

M ....
....
....

A ....
....
....

R ....
....
....

T ....
....

HOW WILL THESE HABITS HELP FULFILL YOUR GOALS?

Habits are notoriously difficult to change or establish, but it's easier to find success when you're crystal clear on how your habits contribute to your goals. In the previous exercise, you reflected on how habits relate to your goals. But because this criterion is so important for your success, it's worth diving in a bit deeper.

Now that you've determined a habit that you want to ditch, change, or improve, consider how this habit will help you lead a life that is more consistent with your values. What value will this habit add to your life?

....
....
....
....

Will this habit still be meaningful many years from now? What goals and values does it support that will continue to be worthwhile long into the future?

....
....
....
....

JOURNAL PROMPTS FOR SUCCESS

The previous exercises helped you learn more about how your chosen habit connects directly to your personal goals and the values that frame your life. Understanding that relationship is key to successfully establishing your new habit. The next section includes more journal prompts that will help you examine your habit at an even deeper level.

You can use a dedicated notebook, a document saved to your computer, or a notes file on your phone to work with the following prompts. You may choose to dive into these prompts now or come back to them as you start to track your daily habits.

1. Habits persist because they are triggered by the environment—people, activities, smells, feelings, and so on. Consider what happens in your life just before you engage in the habit you want to change. What are some of the cues that trigger the habit?

2. Habits are surprisingly difficult to integrate into our lives. For a few days, you can sort of force it. But beyond that, long-term success depends on making some accommodations. You'll need to make some changes in your schedule, in your activities, and in *yourself* to keep this going. What will you have to do or change to make sure the habit becomes and stays a part of your life? Who will you have to become?

3. If we're honest with ourselves, we are one of our biggest obstacles to sustaining new habits. We make excuses, set unrealistic expectations, buy into self-defeating thoughts, or prioritize instant gratification. Consider the ways you might sabotage yourself. What are the biggest impediments to your success?

4. When you're struggling with your habit, you might call yourself names ("lazy," "stupid") or use other disparaging language ("You never get anything right," "This should be easy"). Unfortunately, this type of negative self-talk tends to make it even harder to engage with your habits. Instead, try to develop some positive self-talk you can use whenever you feel the urge to beat yourself up. What encouraging words can you use to motivate yourself the next time you're struggling?

5. The habit you're trying to establish occupies time in your life that was previously occupied by something else. If you simply take up your new habit without adjusting your schedule, you may end up neglecting a need that you used to meet during that time. For instance, let's say the time you are now spending meditating is the time you used to spend cleaning the house. This can keep your habit from being sustainable—when you see how messy your home has gotten, you may decide that the meditation session isn't worth it. But with planning, you can make time for both meditating and cleaning or anything else. What need was being met during the time you're now dedicating to your new habit? How can you still meet that need?

6. Feelings play a major role in how we create and sustain habits. We develop bad habits initially because we want to avoid uncomfortable feelings like stress and anxiety. And it can be hard to set new habits because we have to confront other types of uncomfortable feelings, like uncertainty and frustration, along the way. What feelings do you associate with doing—or not doing—your habit? What coping skills can you use to manage those feelings?

7. Habits are only worthwhile if they add value to your life. This added value could be something like saving you money, enhancing your emotional well-being, or improving your relationships. What value is this habit adding to your life?

8. Once you've spent a little time trying to change your habit, you'll notice that the success you had in the first few days becomes harder to sustain. Perhaps over the first week, you popped out of bed every day at 5 a.m. to hit the gym, but as the weeks went on, you began hitting the snooze button. This is totally normal and simply indicates that you're entering the next phase of your habit-changing journey. What challenges are you encountering? It's important to address those challenges so they don't sabotage your habit entirely. What can you do to overcome those challenges?

9. There will definitely be days when something comes up and interferes with your habit. Even if you have every intention of following through with your habit, you may get sick or have to stay late at work or have a friend who suddenly needs help. Develop a plan for these days. When something comes up that interferes with your normal routine, what is your backup plan for (1) following through with your habit anyway or (2) getting back on track with your habit ASAP?

10. You've spent a lot of time considering why you *want* to add this habit to your life. When you are having trouble sustaining your habit, it's also helpful to consider what happens if you *don't* develop the habit. What will you be missing out on if you don't learn to incorporate this habit into your life? Why should you continue the journey?

TIPS AND TOOLS FOR SUCCESS

Now that you have a solid understanding of the specific habit you're trying to establish or eliminate, you need some evidence-based strategies for success. In part 1, you learned about all the factors that make habits difficult to change, so here are some tips and tools for more success. Read through them now as you're getting started, and review them regularly throughout your journey to refresh your memory.

1. Your brain relies on habits when stress or fatigue depletes your resources, making it harder to make thoughtful choices about your behavior. Set yourself up for success by removing temptations and making the choice easier for your brain. (In other words, make it a no-brainer!) For example, it's easier to limit time on social media when the apps aren't installed on your phone.

2. Your attempt to change your habit is unlikely to be perfectly successful at first. When you reflect on your daily, weekly, and 28-day trackers, expect to see days and even weeks when you struggled. This is totally normal. Unfortunately, your brain isn't particularly motivated to help you change your behavior. Remind yourself that it's normal to encounter a few obstacles and roadblocks as you change your habit. Allow yourself to be imperfect, and focus instead on the progress you're making overall.

3. If at all possible, schedule your habit. Research shows that scheduling an activity—even one you don't necessarily find pleasurable—makes it more likely to happen. Make it easier to engage in your habit on a consistent basis by deciding when you will do it, and then schedule it on your calendar. This ensures that you protect the time you need for your habit and that it doesn't get procrastinated into never happening.

4. If you're having trouble getting your habit established, your goal may be too ambitious. The goal might seem perfectly reasonable, but if your data is showing you that it's tough to be consistent, that tells you it's not quite attainable in your life right now. Try cutting the goal in half—if you've been trying to exercise four days a week and it isn't working, try for two. You could also try focusing on only one goal at a time.

5. Forgetfulness is one of the biggest barriers to establishing and sustaining a new habit. Depending on what type of habit you are trying to establish, you might use alarms or reminders to remember when you want to engage in the habit. Or do the habit as soon as you remember it. For example, if your new habit is to wash dishes more often, commit to washing them the second you pass by a sink full of dishes rather than telling yourself, "Oh, yeah, I'll get to that in an hour or two." Another option is to make the habit as noticeable as possible—if you're trying to sweep the floor more consistently, put the broom where you'll notice it easily.

6. Use imagery to prepare yourself for habits that are a pain to do. Athletes use this skill all the time to run a play before they hit the field. Here's how: Imagine yourself preparing to do the habit, and then imagine yourself doing the habit. Take your time—the more realistic and detailed your visualization is, the more effective it will be. This will mentally prepare your brain to help you engage in the behavior in real life.

7. Sometimes, within just a few seconds of remembering to do a habit, your brain will start trying to talk you out of doing it. This is especially true for habits that are energy-intensive, like exercising. When you notice this happening, ask yourself what choice Future You would want you to make in this moment. Would Future You want you to go to the gym or watch one more episode of your show? Use the answer to take action.

8. Establishing and sustaining habits isn't just about changing your behavior—it's also about managing your feelings. When you're establishing a new habit, you might feel bored, unmotivated, or unsure. Ignoring these feelings will interfere with your habit success, so address them directly. Connect an emotion word to what you're feeling, and cope with it by using a positive affirmation to motivate yourself, reminding yourself that feelings are uncomfortable but not harmful, soothing yourself with some breathing exercises, or using any other of your favorite coping skills.

9. Catch and replace your self-defeating thoughts. If you feel unhelpful thoughts floating through your mind (like "I don't want to do this," "I can't figure this out," "Everyone else can do this—I should be able to, too"), point them out to yourself. Then add a "yet" or "but" to the end of the sentence. Here's how it works: "I don't want to do this" becomes "I don't want to do this, *but* it's important to me and I can do hard things." "I can't figure this out" becomes "I can't figure this out *yet, but* I'm learning from my experience."

10. Recruit a partner to go on your habit journey with you. This will help you remember the habit, increase your motivation to continue with the journey, and enhance your likelihood of accomplishing your goal. Choose someone you trust to check on you consistently and to reorient you if you get off track. Work together to determine rewards for staying on track with your habit.

THINGS TO REMEMBER AS YOU TRACK YOUR HABITS

Although the habit you choose to focus on with this journal is personal, a few key concepts are useful for everyone on a habit-changing journey.

1. The number one mistake people make when starting new habits is that they're too ambitious with their goals, and they try to engage in behaviors that aren't sustainable in the long term. Keep your initial objective small and simple. Find success with something "easy" before you move on to bigger challenges. You'll likely be surprised by how difficult even these seemingly easy changes can be to implement!

2. The number two mistake people make is that they stop monitoring their habit too soon. Once they start feeling a little bit of momentum and success, they ease off the very measures (like tracking and journaling) that were helping them find success. Soon after, their success starts to dwindle. To avoid falling into this trap, keep tracking your behavior *long after* your behavior is firmly established. Keep using the tips and tools in this habit journal for much longer than you believe is really necessary. This will help you sustain your progress.

3. Create as much structure as possible. As we discussed in part 1, habits come from consistently and repeatedly performing a behavior until it becomes automatic. Having a plan for how and when to perform your habit and how to manage obstacles will help you find more consistency. Consider what you will have to do or change to make sure the habit becomes and stays part of your life, and eliminate all the roadblocks you can. When you encounter roadblocks or have moments, days,

or even weeks when your habit slips, be compassionate with yourself. Use the positive affirmations included in this journal to combat self-criticism. Despite the lies your inner critic may tell you, success is more likely to follow encouragement than criticism.

4. Remind yourself that there is no perfect time to start a new habit. There's nothing magical about Monday, the start of the New Year, or the end of the semester that makes it an easier or better time to start a new habit. No matter when you decide to start your new habit, you'll have stress and other priorities competing for your attention. Learning how to manage that is part of establishing new habits. So, remind yourself that today is as good a day as any to start your new habit.

5. Before you start, know that there's nothing easy about establishing a new habit. This habit journal is an evidence-based strategy that will significantly increase your likelihood of success, but there's no quick fix for changing our behavior. Our brains are capable of changing, but these changes don't happen overnight. In addition to consistent effort, it takes *time* to establish a new habit. So, as you set out to change your habits, prepare yourself to work at it consistently (and probably struggle, encounter setbacks, and feel defeated at times) over the course of the journal. Although it's true that simpler habits may develop more quickly and bigger-picture ones may take more time, know that you absolutely can establish new habits with a clear commitment and the right frame of mind.

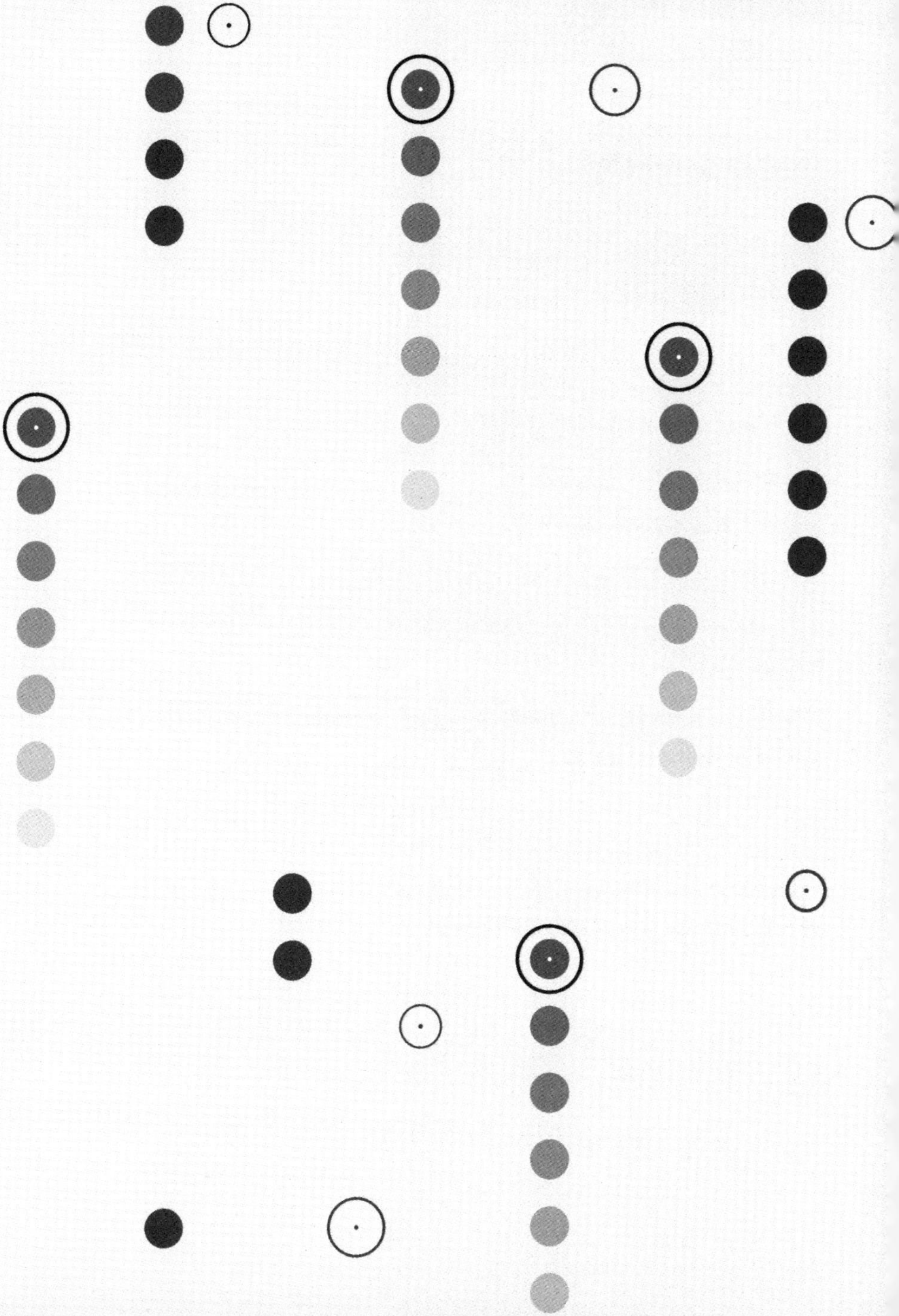

DAILY CHECK-IN — DAY 1

DATE: __ / __ / __

Today I'm grateful for: ....
....
....

Today's habit goal(s): ....
....
....

Habit motivation check:

☐ 1 (I really don't care.)
☐ 2 (This is going to be a challenge.)
☐ 3 (I'm not enthusiastic, but I can do it.)
☐ 4 (I'm feeling confident!)
☐ 5 (I'm excited!)

Mood *(circle one)*: 😃 🙂 😐 🙁 😞

Situations, people, emotions, thoughts, or other behaviors that influenced my habit(s) today: ....
....
....

Daily habit check-in: Write in your habit(s) (such as "Sleep 8 hours") and check off those you stuck with today.

○ .... ○ ....
○ .... ○ ....
○ .... ○ ....
○ .... ○ ....
○ .... ○ ....

DAILY CHECK-IN **DAY 2**

DATE: ___ / ___ / ___

Today I'm grateful for: ....
....
....

Today's habit goal(s): ....
....
....

Habit motivation check:

☐ 1 (I really don't care.)
☐ 2 (This is going to be a challenge.)
☐ 3 (I'm not enthusiastic, but I can do it.)
☐ 4 (I'm feeling confident!)
☐ 5 (I'm excited!)

Mood *(circle one)*: 😀 🙂 😐 🙁 😫

Situations, people, emotions, thoughts, or other behaviors that influenced my habit(s) today: ....
....
....

Daily habit check-in: Write in your habit(s) (such as "Sleep 8 hours") and check off those you stuck with today.

○ ....   ○ ....
○ ....   ○ ....
○ ....   ○ ....
○ ....   ○ ....
○ ....   ○ ....

DAILY CHECK-IN (DAY 3)

DATE: ___/___/___

Today I'm grateful for: ....
....
....

Today's habit goal(s): ....
....
....

Habit motivation check:

☐ 1 (I really don't care.)
☐ 2 (This is going to be a challenge.)
☐ 3 (I'm not enthusiastic, but I can do it.)
☐ 4 (I'm feeling confident!)
☐ 5 (I'm excited!)

Mood *(circle one):* 😀 🙂 😐 🙁 😫

Situations, people, emotions, thoughts, or other behaviors that influenced my habit(s) today: ....
....
....

Daily habit check-in: Write in your habit(s) (such as "Sleep 8 hours") and check off those you stuck with today.

○ .... ○ ....
○ .... ○ ....
○ .... ○ ....
○ .... ○ ....
○ .... ○ ....

DAILY CHECK-IN (DAY 4)

DATE: __/__/__

Today I'm grateful for: ....
....
....

Today's habit goal(s): ....
....
....

Habit motivation check:

☐ 1 (I really don't care.)
☐ 2 (This is going to be a challenge.)
☐ 3 (I'm not enthusiastic, but I can do it.)
☐ 4 (I'm feeling confident!)
☐ 5 (I'm excited!)

Mood *(circle one)*: 😀 🙂 😐 🙁 😫

Situations, people, emotions, thoughts, or other behaviors that influenced my habit(s) today: ....
....
....

Daily habit check-in: Write in your habit(s) (such as "Sleep 8 hours") and check off those you stuck with today.

○ ....   ○ ....
○ ....   ○ ....
○ ....   ○ ....
○ ....   ○ ....
○ ....   ○ ....

DAILY CHECK-IN (DAY 5)

DATE: __ / __ / __

Today I'm grateful for: ....
....
....

Today's habit goal(s): ....
....
....

Habit motivation check:

☐ 1 (I really don't care.)
☐ 2 (This is going to be a challenge.)
☐ 3 (I'm not enthusiastic, but I can do it.)
☐ 4 (I'm feeling confident!)
☐ 5 (I'm excited!)

Mood *(circle one)*: 😃 🙂 😐 🙁 ☹️

Situations, people, emotions, thoughts, or other behaviors that influenced my habit(s) today: ....
....
....

Daily habit check-in: Write in your habit(s) (such as "Sleep 8 hours") and check off those you stuck with today.

○ .... ○ ....
○ .... ○ ....
○ .... ○ ....
○ .... ○ ....
○ .... ○ ....

DAILY CHECK-IN (DAY 6)

DATE: __/__/__

Today I'm grateful for: ....
....
....

Today's habit goal(s): ....
....
....

Habit motivation check:

☐ 1 (I really don't care.)
☐ 2 (This is going to be a challenge.)
☐ 3 (I'm not enthusiastic, but I can do it.)
☐ 4 (I'm feeling confident!)
☐ 5 (I'm excited!)

Mood *(circle one)*: 😀 🙂 😐 🙁 😣

Situations, people, emotions, thoughts, or other behaviors that influenced my habit(s) today: ....
....
....

Daily habit check-in: Write in your habit(s) (such as "Sleep 8 hours") and check off those you stuck with today.

○	○ ....
○	○ ....
○	○ ....
○	○ ....
○	○ ....

DAILY CHECK-IN (DAY 7)

DATE: __/__/__

Today I'm grateful for: ....
....
....

Today's habit goal(s): ....
....
....

Habit motivation check:

- ☐ 1 (I really don't care.)
- ☐ 2 (This is going to be a challenge.)
- ☐ 3 (I'm not enthusiastic, but I can do it.)
- ☐ 4 (I'm feeling confident!)
- ☐ 5 (I'm excited!)

Mood *(circle one)*: 😃 🙂 😐 🙁 😣

Situations, people, emotions, thoughts, or other behaviors that influenced my habit(s) today: ....
....
....

Daily habit check-in: Write in your habit(s) (such as "Sleep 8 hours") and check off those you stuck with today.

- ○ ....
- ○ ....
- ○ ....
- ○ ....
- ○ ....
- ○ ....
- ○ ....
- ○ ....
- ○ ....
- ○ ....

WEEKLY CHECK-IN `WEEK 1`

DATE: ___/___/___

This week's habit goal(s): ....
....
....

What went well this week with my habit(s): ....
....
....

Where I struggled this week with my habit(s): ....
....
....

What thoughts, feelings, or situations influenced my habit(s) this week:
....
....

What I plan to modify for next week: ....
....
....

Advantages of sticking with my habit(s) this week: ....
....
....

Next week's habit goal(s): ....
....
....

> "You'll never change your life until you change something you do daily. The secret of your success is found in your daily routine." —JOHN C. MAXWELL

DAILY CHECK-IN (DAY 8)

DATE: __/__/__

Today I'm grateful for: ....
....
....

Today's habit goal(s): ....
....
....

Habit motivation check:

☐ 1 (I really don't care.)
☐ 2 (This is going to be a challenge.)
☐ 3 (I'm not enthusiastic, but I can do it.)
☐ 4 (I'm feeling confident!)
☐ 5 (I'm excited!)

Mood *(circle one)*: 😀 🙂 😐 🙁 😢

Situations, people, emotions, thoughts, or other behaviors that influenced my habit(s) today: ....
....
....

Daily habit check-in: Write in your habit(s) (such as "Sleep 8 hours") and check off those you stuck with today.

○ .... ○ ....
○ .... ○ ....
○ .... ○ ....
○ .... ○ ....
○ .... ○ ....

DAILY CHECK-IN (DAY 9)

DATE: / /

Today I'm grateful for: ....
....
....

Today's habit goal(s): ....
....
....

Habit motivation check:

- ☐ 1 (I really don't care.)
- ☐ 2 (This is going to be a challenge.)
- ☐ 3 (I'm not enthusiastic, but I can do it.)
- ☐ 4 (I'm feeling confident!)
- ☐ 5 (I'm excited!)

Mood *(circle one)*: 😃 🙂 😐 🙁 😩

Situations, people, emotions, thoughts, or other behaviors that influenced my habit(s) today: ....
....
....

Daily habit check-in: Write in your habit(s) (such as "Sleep 8 hours") and check off those you stuck with today.

○	○ ....
○	○ ....
○	○ ....
○	○ ....
○	○ ....

UNDERSTAND AND TRACK YOUR HABITS

DAILY CHECK-IN (DAY 10)

DATE: __/ /__

Today I'm grateful for: ....
....
....

Today's habit goal(s): ....
....
....

Habit motivation check:

☐ 1 (I really don't care.)
☐ 2 (This is going to be a challenge.)
☐ 3 (I'm not enthusiastic, but I can do it.)
☐ 4 (I'm feeling confident!)
☐ 5 (I'm excited!)

Mood *(circle one)*: 😃 🙂 😐 🙁 😣

Situations, people, emotions, thoughts, or other behaviors that influenced my habit(s) today: ....
....
....

Daily habit check-in: Write in your habit(s) (such as "Sleep 8 hours") and check off those you stuck with today.

○ .... ○ ....
○ .... ○ ....
○ .... ○ ....
○ .... ○ ....
○ .... ○ ....

44 THE EASY HABITS JOURNAL

DAILY CHECK-IN (DAY 11)

DATE: ...... / ...... / ......

Today I'm grateful for: ......

Today's habit goal(s): ......

Habit motivation check:

☐ 1 (I really don't care.)
☐ 2 (This is going to be a challenge.)
☐ 3 (I'm not enthusiastic, but I can do it.)
☐ 4 (I'm feeling confident!)
☐ 5 (I'm excited!)

Mood *(circle one)*: 😃 🙂 😐 🙁 😫

Situations, people, emotions, thoughts, or other behaviors that influenced my habit(s) today: ......

Daily habit check-in: Write in your habit(s) (such as "Sleep 8 hours") and check off those you stuck with today.

○ ...... ○ ......
○ ...... ○ ......
○ ...... ○ ......
○ ...... ○ ......
○ ...... ○ ......

DAILY CHECK-IN — DAY 12

DATE: __/__/__

Today I'm grateful for: ....
....
....

Today's habit goal(s): ....
....
....

Habit motivation check:

☐ 1 (I really don't care.)
☐ 2 (This is going to be a challenge.)
☐ 3 (I'm not enthusiastic, but I can do it.)
☐ 4 (I'm feeling confident!)
☐ 5 (I'm excited!)

Mood *(circle one)*: 😃 🙂 😐 🙁 😫

Situations, people, emotions, thoughts, or other behaviors that influenced my habit(s) today: ....
....
....

Daily habit check-in: Write in your habit(s) (such as "Sleep 8 hours") and check off those you stuck with today.

○ .... ○ ....
○ .... ○ ....
○ .... ○ ....
○ .... ○ ....
○ .... ○ ....

DAILY CHECK-IN (DAY 13)

DATE: ___/___/___

Today I'm grateful for: ....
....
....

Today's habit goal(s): ....
....
....

Habit motivation check:

- ☐ 1 (I really don't care.)
- ☐ 2 (This is going to be a challenge.)
- ☐ 3 (I'm not enthusiastic, but I can do it.)
- ☐ 4 (I'm feeling confident!)
- ☐ 5 (I'm excited!)

Mood *(circle one)*: 😀 🙂 😐 🙁 😫

Situations, people, emotions, thoughts, or other behaviors that influenced my habit(s) today: ....
....
....

Daily habit check-in: Write in your habit(s) (such as "Sleep 8 hours") and check off those you stuck with today.

- ○ ....
- ○ ....
- ○ ....
- ○ ....
- ○ ....
- ○ ....
- ○ ....
- ○ ....
- ○ ....
- ○ ....

DAILY CHECK-IN (DAY 14)

DATE: / /

Today I'm grateful for: ....
....
....

Today's habit goal(s): ....
....
....

Habit motivation check:

- ☐ 1 (I really don't care.)
- ☐ 2 (This is going to be a challenge.)
- ☐ 3 (I'm not enthusiastic, but I can do it.)
- ☐ 4 (I'm feeling confident!)
- ☐ 5 (I'm excited!)

Mood (circle one): 😃 🙂 😐 🙁 😫

Situations, people, emotions, thoughts, or other behaviors that influenced my habit(s) today: ....
....
....

Daily habit check-in: Write in your habit(s) (such as "Sleep 8 hours") and check off those you stuck with today.

○ .... ○ ....
○ .... ○ ....
○ .... ○ ....
○ .... ○ ....
○ .... ○ ....

WEEKLY CHECK-IN `WEEK 2`

DATE: ___ / ___ / ___

This week's habit goal(s): ....
....
....

What went well this week with my habit(s): ....
....
....

Where I struggled this week with my habit(s): ....
....
....

What thoughts, feelings, or situations influenced my habit(s) this week:
....
....

What I plan to modify for next week: ....
....
....

Advantages of sticking with my habit(s) this week: ....
....
....

Next week's habit goal(s): ....
....
....

> I will take consistent, imperfect
> steps toward my goals.

DAILY CHECK-IN (DAY 15)

DATE: / /

Today I'm grateful for: ....
....
....

Today's habit goal(s): ....
....
....

Habit motivation check:

☐ 1 (I really don't care.)
☐ 2 (This is going to be a challenge.)
☐ 3 (I'm not enthusiastic, but I can do it.)
☐ 4 (I'm feeling confident!)
☐ 5 (I'm excited!)

Mood *(circle one)*: 😃 🙂 😐 🙁 😫

Situations, people, emotions, thoughts, or other behaviors that influenced my habit(s) today: ....
....
....

Daily habit check-in: Write in your habit(s) (such as "Sleep 8 hours") and check off those you stuck with today.

○ .... ○ ....
○ .... ○ ....
○ .... ○ ....
○ .... ○ ....
○ .... ○ ....

THE EASY HABITS JOURNAL

DAILY CHECK-IN (DAY 16)

DATE: __ / __ / __

Today I'm grateful for: ....
....
....

Today's habit goal(s): ....
....
....

Habit motivation check:

- [ ] 1 (I really don't care.)
- [ ] 2 (This is going to be a challenge.)
- [ ] 3 (I'm not enthusiastic, but I can do it.)
- [ ] 4 (I'm feeling confident!)
- [ ] 5 (I'm excited!)

Mood *(circle one)*: 😃 🙂 😐 🙁 😣

Situations, people, emotions, thoughts, or other behaviors that influenced my habit(s) today: ....
....
....

Daily habit check-in: Write in your habit(s) (such as "Sleep 8 hours") and check off those you stuck with today.

- ○ ....
- ○ ....
- ○ ....
- ○ ....
- ○ ....
- ○ ....
- ○ ....
- ○ ....
- ○ ....
- ○ ....

DAILY CHECK-IN — DAY 17

DATE: ___/___/___

Today I'm grateful for: ....
....
....

Today's habit goal(s): ....
....
....

Habit motivation check:

☐ 1 (I really don't care.)
☐ 2 (This is going to be a challenge.)
☐ 3 (I'm not enthusiastic, but I can do it.)
☐ 4 (I'm feeling confident!)
☐ 5 (I'm excited!)

Mood *(circle one)*: 😀 🙂 😐 🙁 😫

Situations, people, emotions, thoughts, or other behaviors that influenced my habit(s) today: ....
....
....

Daily habit check-in: Write in your habit(s) (such as "Sleep 8 hours") and check off those you stuck with today.

○ ....   ○ ....
○ ....   ○ ....
○ ....   ○ ....
○ ....   ○ ....
○ ....   ○ ....

DAILY CHECK-IN (DAY 18)

DATE: __/__/__

Today I'm grateful for: ....
....
....

Today's habit goal(s): ....
....
....

Habit motivation check:

☐ 1 (I really don't care.)
☐ 2 (This is going to be a challenge.)
☐ 3 (I'm not enthusiastic, but I can do it.)
☐ 4 (I'm feeling confident!)
☐ 5 (I'm excited!)

Mood *(circle one)*: 😃 🙂 😐 🙁 😣

Situations, people, emotions, thoughts, or other behaviors that influenced my habit(s) today: ....
....
....

Daily habit check-in: Write in your habit(s) (such as "Sleep 8 hours") and check off those you stuck with today.

○ .... ○ ....
○ .... ○ ....
○ .... ○ ....
○ .... ○ ....
○ .... ○ ....

DAILY CHECK-IN (DAY 19)

DATE: __ / __ / __

Today I'm grateful for: ....
....
....

Today's habit goal(s): ....
....
....

Habit motivation check:

☐ 1 (I really don't care.)
☐ 2 (This is going to be a challenge.)
☐ 3 (I'm not enthusiastic, but I can do it.)
☐ 4 (I'm feeling confident!)
☐ 5 (I'm excited!)

Mood *(circle one)*: 😃 🙂 😐 🙁 😫

Situations, people, emotions, thoughts, or other behaviors that influenced my habit(s) today: ....
....
....

Daily habit check-in: Write in your habit(s) (such as "Sleep 8 hours") and check off those you stuck with today.

○ ....   ○ ....
○ ....   ○ ....
○ ....   ○ ....
○ ....   ○ ....
○ ....   ○ ....

DAILY CHECK-IN (DAY 20)

DATE: __/__/__

Today I'm grateful for: ....
....
....

Today's habit goal(s): ....
....
....

Habit motivation check:

☐ 1 (I really don't care.)
☐ 2 (This is going to be a challenge.)
☐ 3 (I'm not enthusiastic, but I can do it.)
☐ 4 (I'm feeling confident!)
☐ 5 (I'm excited!)

Mood *(circle one)*: 😃 🙂 😐 🙁 😫

Situations, people, emotions, thoughts, or other behaviors that influenced my habit(s) today: ....
....
....

Daily habit check-in: Write in your habit(s) (such as "Sleep 8 hours") and check off those you stuck with today.

○ ....   ○ ....
○ ....   ○ ....
○ ....   ○ ....
○ ....   ○ ....
○ ....   ○ ....

UNDERSTAND AND TRACK YOUR HABITS

DAILY CHECK-IN (DAY 21)

DATE: / /

Today I'm grateful for: ....
....
....

Today's habit goal(s): ....
....
....

Habit motivation check:

☐ 1 (I really don't care.)
☐ 2 (This is going to be a challenge.)
☐ 3 (I'm not enthusiastic, but I can do it.)
☐ 4 (I'm feeling confident!)
☐ 5 (I'm excited!)

Mood *(circle one)*: 😃 🙂 😐 🙁 😫

Situations, people, emotions, thoughts, or other behaviors that influenced my habit(s) today: ....
....
....

Daily habit check-in: Write in your habit(s) (such as "Sleep 8 hours") and check off those you stuck with today.

○ .... ○ ....
○ .... ○ ....
○ .... ○ ....
○ .... ○ ....
○ .... ○ ....

WEEKLY CHECK-IN `WEEK 3`

DATE: ___/___/___

This week's habit goal(s): ....

What went well this week with my habit(s): ....

Where I struggled this week with my habit(s): ....

What thoughts, feelings, or situations influenced my habit(s) this week:

What I plan to modify for next week: ....

Advantages of sticking with my habit(s) this week: ....

Next week's habit goal(s): ....

> "Changing a habit or instigating something new is toughest at the start. Through repetition, however, new habits grow. They are strengthened in the course of familiarity." —RICHELLE E. GOODRICH

UNDERSTAND AND TRACK YOUR HABITS

DAILY CHECK-IN (DAY 22)

DATE: ___/___/___

Today I'm grateful for: ....
....
....

Today's habit goal(s): ....
....
....

Habit motivation check:

☐ 1 (I really don't care.)
☐ 2 (This is going to be a challenge.)
☐ 3 (I'm not enthusiastic, but I can do it.)
☐ 4 (I'm feeling confident!)
☐ 5 (I'm excited!)

Mood *(circle one)*: 😀 🙂 😐 🙁 😣

Situations, people, emotions, thoughts, or other behaviors that influenced my habit(s) today: ....
....
....

Daily habit check-in: Write in your habit(s) (such as "Sleep 8 hours") and check off those you stuck with today.

○ .... ○ ....
○ .... ○ ....
○ .... ○ ....
○ .... ○ ....
○ .... ○ ....

DAILY CHECK-IN — DAY 23

DATE: ___ / ___ / ___

Today I'm grateful for: ....
....
....

Today's habit goal(s): ....
....
....

Habit motivation check:

☐ 1 (I really don't care.)
☐ 2 (This is going to be a challenge.)
☐ 3 (I'm not enthusiastic, but I can do it.)
☐ 4 (I'm feeling confident!)
☐ 5 (I'm excited!)

Mood *(circle one)*: 😄 🙂 😐 🙁 😫

Situations, people, emotions, thoughts, or other behaviors that influenced my habit(s) today: ....
....
....

Daily habit check-in: Write in your habit(s) (such as "Sleep 8 hours") and check off those you stuck with today.

○ ....   ○ ....
○ ....   ○ ....
○ ....   ○ ....
○ ....   ○ ....
○ ....   ○ ....

DAILY CHECK-IN (DAY 24)

DATE: ___/___/___

Today I'm grateful for: ....
....
....

Today's habit goal(s): ....
....
....

Habit motivation check:

☐ 1 (I really don't care.)
☐ 2 (This is going to be a challenge.)
☐ 3 (I'm not enthusiastic, but I can do it.)
☐ 4 (I'm feeling confident!)
☐ 5 (I'm excited!)

Mood *(circle one)*: 😃 🙂 😐 🙁 😣

Situations, people, emotions, thoughts, or other behaviors that influenced my habit(s) today: ....
....
....

Daily habit check-in: Write in your habit(s) (such as "Sleep 8 hours") and check off those you stuck with today.

○ .... ○ ....
○ .... ○ ....
○ .... ○ ....
○ .... ○ ....
○ .... ○ ....

DAILY CHECK-IN | DAY 25

DATE: ___ / ___ / ___

Today I'm grateful for: ....

....

....

Today's habit goal(s): ....

....

....

Habit motivation check:

☐ 1 (I really don't care.)
☐ 2 (This is going to be a challenge.)
☐ 3 (I'm not enthusiastic, but I can do it.)
☐ 4 (I'm feeling confident!)
☐ 5 (I'm excited!)

Mood *(circle one)*: 😃 🙂 😐 🙁 😫

Situations, people, emotions, thoughts, or other behaviors that influenced my habit(s) today: ....

....

....

Daily habit check-in: Write in your habit(s) (such as "Sleep 8 hours") and check off those you stuck with today.

○ ....   ○ ....
○ ....   ○ ....
○ ....   ○ ....
○ ....   ○ ....
○ ....   ○ ....

UNDERSTAND AND TRACK YOUR HABITS

DAILY CHECK-IN — DAY 26

DATE: ___/___/___

Today I'm grateful for: ....
....
....

Today's habit goal(s): ....
....
....

Habit motivation check:

☐ 1 (I really don't care.)
☐ 2 (This is going to be a challenge.)
☐ 3 (I'm not enthusiastic, but I can do it.)
☐ 4 (I'm feeling confident!)
☐ 5 (I'm excited!)

Mood *(circle one)*: 😃 🙂 😐 🙁 😣

Situations, people, emotions, thoughts, or other behaviors that influenced my habit(s) today: ....
....
....

Daily habit check-in: Write in your habit(s) (such as "Sleep 8 hours") and check off those you stuck with today.

○ ....   ○ ....
○ ....   ○ ....
○ ....   ○ ....
○ ....   ○ ....
○ ....   ○ ....

DAILY CHECK-IN (DAY 27)

DATE: __ / __ / __

Today I'm grateful for: ....
....
....

Today's habit goal(s): ....
....
....

Habit motivation check:

☐ 1 (I really don't care.)
☐ 2 (This is going to be a challenge.)
☐ 3 (I'm not enthusiastic, but I can do it.)
☐ 4 (I'm feeling confident!)
☐ 5 (I'm excited!)

Mood *(circle one)*: 😄 🙂 😐 🙁 😣

Situations, people, emotions, thoughts, or other behaviors that influenced my habit(s) today: ....
....
....

Daily habit check-in: Write in your habit(s) (such as "Sleep 8 hours") and check off those you stuck with today.

○ .... ○ ....
○ .... ○ ....
○ .... ○ ....
○ .... ○ ....
○ .... ○ ....

UNDERSTAND AND TRACK YOUR HABITS

DAILY CHECK-IN | DAY 28

DATE: /   /

Today I'm grateful for: ....
....
....

Today's habit goal(s): ....
....
....

Habit motivation check:

☐ 1 (I really don't care.)
☐ 2 (This is going to be a challenge.)
☐ 3 (I'm not enthusiastic, but I can do it.)
☐ 4 (I'm feeling confident!)
☐ 5 (I'm excited!)

Mood *(circle one)*: 😃 🙂 😐 🙁 😣

Situations, people, emotions, thoughts, or other behaviors that influenced my habit(s) today: ....
....
....

Daily habit check-in: Write in your habit(s) (such as "Sleep 8 hours") and check off those you stuck with today.

○ ....   ○ ....
○ ....   ○ ....
○ ....   ○ ....
○ ....   ○ ....
○ ....   ○ ....

WEEKLY CHECK-IN `WEEK 4`

DATE: __/__/__

This week's habit goal(s): ....
....

What went well this week with my habit(s): ....
....

Where I struggled this week with my habit(s): ....
....

What thoughts, feelings, or situations influenced my habit(s) this week:
....
....

What I plan to modify for next week: ....
....

Advantages of sticking with my habit(s) this week: ....
....

Next week's habit goal(s): ....
....

> "It's not about perfect. It's about effort. And when you bring that effort every single day, that's where transformation happens. That's how change occurs." —**JILLIAN MICHAELS**

28-DAY CHECK-IN   DATE: __ / __ / __

My habit goal(s) for this 28-day period: ....

How often I was performing my habit(s) at the start of the last 28 days:
....

How often I am performing my habit(s) now: ....

I am making progress: ☐ Yes   ☐ No   ☐ It's complicated: ....

What went well with my habit(s) over the 28 days: ....
....

Where I struggled with my habit(s) over the 28 days: ....
....

What thoughts, feelings, or situations influenced my habit(s) over the 28 days: ....

What I plan to modify for the next 28 days: ....
....

My habit goal(s) for the next 28 days: ....
....

Future behavior is predicted by past behavior.
The past starts today.

66 THE EASY HABITS JOURNAL

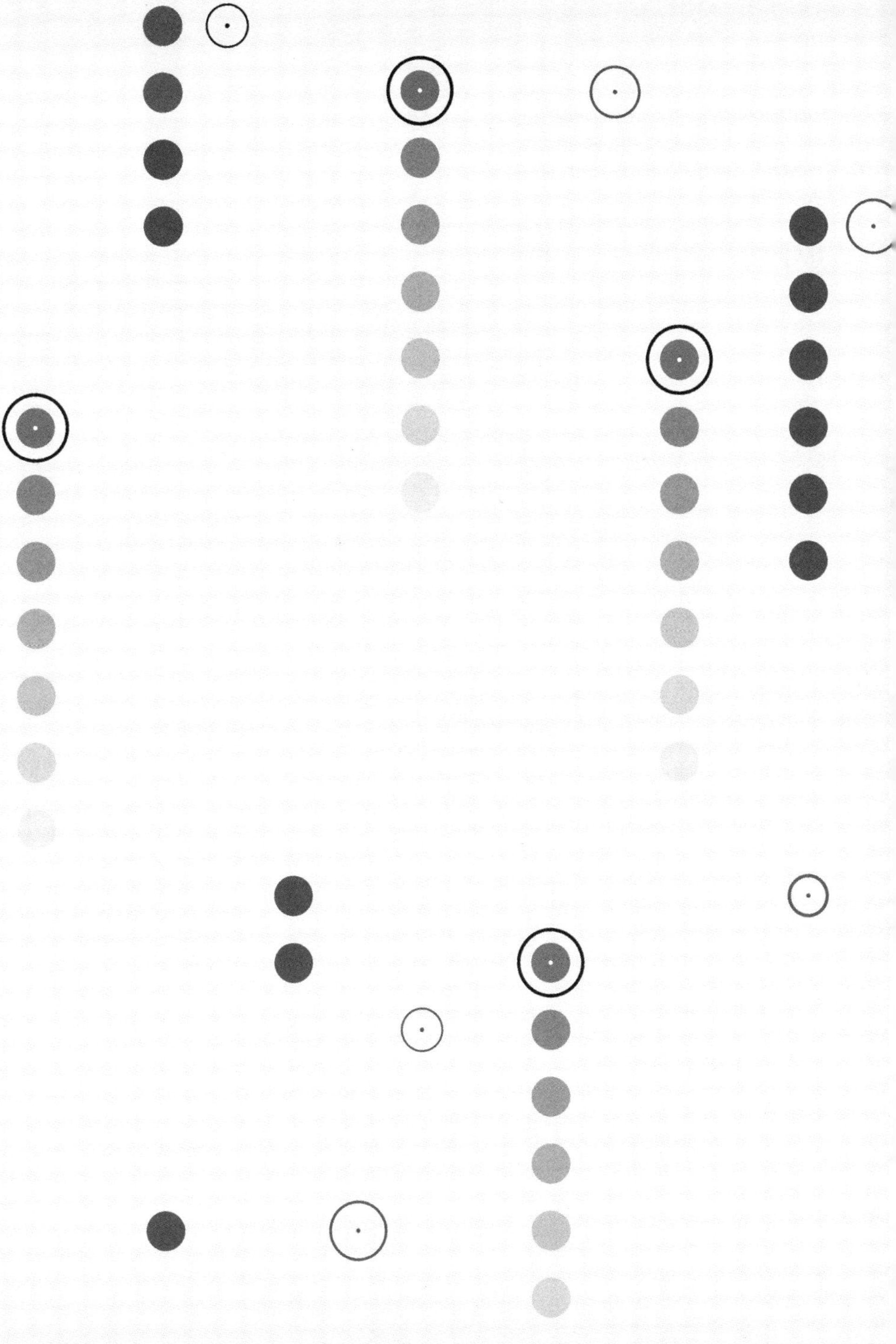

28-DAY HABIT CHART

Let's see how you went over the past 28 days. First, write down three of the key habits you tried to establish.

HABIT 1..................................

HABIT 2..................................

HABIT 3..................................

Then check which days you practiced them in the table.

	HABIT 1	HABIT 2	HABIT 3
DAY 1			
DAY 2			
DAY 3			
DAY 4			
DAY 5			
DAY 6			
DAY 7			
DAY 8			
DAY 9			
DAY 10			
DAY 11			
DAY 12			
DAY 13			
DAY 14			
DAY 15			
DAY 16			
DAY 17			
DAY 18			
DAY 19			
DAY 20			
DAY 21			
DAY 22			
DAY 23			
DAY 24			
DAY 25			
DAY 26			
DAY 27			
DAY 28			

28-DAY HABIT CHART

	HABIT 1	HABIT 2	HABIT 3
Completed streaks/days			
Goal streaks/days to complete			

Why I'm committed to these habits
How these habits reflect my goals and core values

....

....

....

....

Obstacles I might encounter   How I'll manage those obstacles

....

....

....

....

Notes about my habits that will be helpful for the next 28 days

....

....

....

....

"We all make mistakes, have struggles, and even regret things in our past. But you are not your mistakes, you are not your struggles, and you are here NOW with the power to shape your day and your future." —STEVE MARABOLI

DAILY CHECK-IN (DAY 29)

DATE: __ / __ / __

Today I'm grateful for: ....
....
....

Today's habit goal(s): ....
....
....

Habit motivation check:

☐ 1 (I really don't care.)
☐ 2 (This is going to be a challenge.)
☐ 3 (I'm not enthusiastic, but I can do it.)
☐ 4 (I'm feeling confident!)
☐ 5 (I'm excited!)

Mood *(circle one)*: 😃 🙂 😐 🙁 😣

Situations, people, emotions, thoughts, or other behaviors that influenced my habit(s) today: ....
....
....

Daily habit check-in: Write in your habit(s) (such as "Sleep 8 hours") and check off those you stuck with today.

○ .... ○ ....
○ .... ○ ....
○ .... ○ ....
○ .... ○ ....
○ .... ○ ....

DAILY CHECK-IN (DAY 30)

DATE: ___/___/___

Today I'm grateful for: ....
....
....

Today's habit goal(s): ....
....
....

Habit motivation check:

- [ ] 1 (I really don't care.)
- [ ] 2 (This is going to be a challenge.)
- [ ] 3 (I'm not enthusiastic, but I can do it.)
- [ ] 4 (I'm feeling confident!)
- [ ] 5 (I'm excited!)

Mood *(circle one)*: 😃 🙂 😐 🙁 😫

Situations, people, emotions, thoughts, or other behaviors that influenced my habit(s) today: ....
....
....

Daily habit check-in: Write in your habit(s) (such as "Sleep 8 hours") and check off those you stuck with today.

- ○ ....   ○ ....
- ○ ....   ○ ....
- ○ ....   ○ ....
- ○ ....   ○ ....
- ○ ....   ○ ....

DAILY CHECK-IN — DAY 31

DATE: __ / __ / __

Today I'm grateful for: ....
....
....

Today's habit goal(s): ....
....
....

Habit motivation check:

☐ 1 (I really don't care.)
☐ 2 (This is going to be a challenge.)
☐ 3 (I'm not enthusiastic, but I can do it.)
☐ 4 (I'm feeling confident!)
☐ 5 (I'm excited!)

Mood *(circle one)*: 😀 🙂 😐 🙁 😣

Situations, people, emotions, thoughts, or other behaviors that influenced my habit(s) today: ....
....
....

Daily habit check-in: Write in your habit(s) (such as "Sleep 8 hours") and check off those you stuck with today.

○ ....   ○ ....
○ ....   ○ ....
○ ....   ○ ....
○ ....   ○ ....
○ ....   ○ ....

DAILY CHECK-IN

DAY 32

DATE: __ / __ / __

Today I'm grateful for: ....
....
....

Today's habit goal(s): ....
....
....

Habit motivation check:

☐ 1 (I really don't care.)
☐ 2 (This is going to be a challenge.)
☐ 3 (I'm not enthusiastic, but I can do it.)
☐ 4 (I'm feeling confident!)
☐ 5 (I'm excited!)

Mood *(circle one)*: 😃 🙂 😐 🙁 😖

Situations, people, emotions, thoughts, or other behaviors that influenced my habit(s) today: ....
....
....

Daily habit check-in: Write in your habit(s) (such as "Sleep 8 hours") and check off those you stuck with today.

○ .... ○ ....
○ .... ○ ....
○ .... ○ ....
○ .... ○ ....
○ .... ○ ....

DAILY CHECK-IN (DAY 33)

DATE: __ / __ / __

Today I'm grateful for: ....
....
....

Today's habit goal(s): ....
....
....

Habit motivation check:

☐ 1 (I really don't care.)
☐ 2 (This is going to be a challenge.)
☐ 3 (I'm not enthusiastic, but I can do it.)
☐ 4 (I'm feeling confident!)
☐ 5 (I'm excited!)

Mood *(circle one)*: 😀 🙂 😐 🙁 😣

Situations, people, emotions, thoughts, or other behaviors that influenced my habit(s) today: ....
....
....

Daily habit check-in: Write in your habit(s) (such as "Sleep 8 hours") and check off those you stuck with today.

○ .... ○ ....
○ .... ○ ....
○ .... ○ ....
○ .... ○ ....
○ .... ○ ....

74 THE EASY HABITS JOURNAL

DAILY CHECK-IN — DAY 34

DATE: / /

Today I'm grateful for: ....
....
....

Today's habit goal(s): ....
....
....

Habit motivation check:

- [ ] 1 (I really don't care.)
- [ ] 2 (This is going to be a challenge.)
- [ ] 3 (I'm not enthusiastic, but I can do it.)
- [ ] 4 (I'm feeling confident!)
- [ ] 5 (I'm excited!)

Mood *(circle one)*: 😃 🙂 😐 🙁 😣

Situations, people, emotions, thoughts, or other behaviors that influenced my habit(s) today: ....
....
....

Daily habit check-in: Write in your habit(s) (such as "Sleep 8 hours") and check off those you stuck with today.

○	....	○	....
○	....	○	....
○	....	○	....
○	....	○	....
○	....	○	....

DAILY CHECK-IN (DAY 35)

DATE: / /

Today I'm grateful for: ....
....
....

Today's habit goal(s): ....
....
....

Habit motivation check:

☐ 1 (I really don't care.)
☐ 2 (This is going to be a challenge.)
☐ 3 (I'm not enthusiastic, but I can do it.)
☐ 4 (I'm feeling confident!)
☐ 5 (I'm excited!)

Mood *(circle one)*: 😃 🙂 😐 🙁 😣

Situations, people, emotions, thoughts, or other behaviors that influenced my habit(s) today: ....
....
....

Daily habit check-in: Write in your habit(s) (such as "Sleep 8 hours") and check off those you stuck with today.

○ .... ○ ....
○ .... ○ ....
○ .... ○ ....
○ .... ○ ....
○ .... ○ ....

WEEKLY CHECK-IN `WEEK 5`

DATE: ___ / ___ / ___

This week's habit goal(s): ....
....
....

What went well this week with my habit(s): ....
....
....

Where I struggled this week with my habit(s): ....
....
....

What thoughts, feelings, or situations influenced my habit(s) this week:
....
....

What I plan to modify for next week: ....
....
....

Advantages of sticking with my habit(s) this week: ....
....
....

Next week's habit goal(s): ....
....
....

> "What you do every day matters more than what you do once in a while." — GRETCHEN RUBIN

DAILY CHECK-IN (DAY 36)

DATE: / /

Today I'm grateful for: ....
....
....

Today's habit goal(s): ....
....
....

Habit motivation check:

☐ 1 (I really don't care.)
☐ 2 (This is going to be a challenge.)
☐ 3 (I'm not enthusiastic, but I can do it.)
☐ 4 (I'm feeling confident!)
☐ 5 (I'm excited!)

Mood *(circle one)*: 😃 🙂 😐 🙁 ☹️

Situations, people, emotions, thoughts, or other behaviors that influenced my habit(s) today: ....
....
....

Daily habit check-in: Write in your habit(s) (such as "Sleep 8 hours") and check off those you stuck with today.

○ ....   ○ ....
○ ....   ○ ....
○ ....   ○ ....
○ ....   ○ ....
○ ....   ○ ....

78 THE EASY HABITS JOURNAL

DAILY CHECK-IN — DAY 37

DATE: ___ / ___ / ___

Today I'm grateful for: ....

....

....

Today's habit goal(s): ....

....

....

Habit motivation check:

☐ 1 (I really don't care.)
☐ 2 (This is going to be a challenge.)
☐ 3 (I'm not enthusiastic, but I can do it.)
☐ 4 (I'm feeling confident!)
☐ 5 (I'm excited!)

Mood *(circle one)*: 😃 🙂 😐 🙁 😣

Situations, people, emotions, thoughts, or other behaviors that influenced my habit(s) today: ....

....

....

Daily habit check-in: Write in your habit(s) (such as "Sleep 8 hours") and check off those you stuck with today.

○ .... ○ ....
○ .... ○ ....
○ .... ○ ....
○ .... ○ ....
○ .... ○ ....

DAILY CHECK-IN (DAY 38)

DATE: __ / __ / __

Today I'm grateful for: ....
....
....

Today's habit goal(s): ....
....
....

Habit motivation check:

☐ 1 (I really don't care.)
☐ 2 (This is going to be a challenge.)
☐ 3 (I'm not enthusiastic, but I can do it.)
☐ 4 (I'm feeling confident!)
☐ 5 (I'm excited!)

Mood *(circle one)*: 😃 🙂 😐 🙁 😫

Situations, people, emotions, thoughts, or other behaviors that influenced my habit(s) today: ....
....
....

Daily habit check-in: Write in your habit(s) (such as "Sleep 8 hours") and check off those you stuck with today.

○ .... ○ ....
○ .... ○ ....
○ .... ○ ....
○ .... ○ ....
○ .... ○ ....

DAILY CHECK-IN (DAY 39)

DATE: __ / __ / __

Today I'm grateful for: _____
_____
_____

Today's habit goal(s): _____
_____
_____

Habit motivation check:

☐ 1 (I really don't care.)
☐ 2 (This is going to be a challenge.)
☐ 3 (I'm not enthusiastic, but I can do it.)
☐ 4 (I'm feeling confident!)
☐ 5 (I'm excited!)

Mood *(circle one)*: 😃 🙂 😐 🙁 😣

Situations, people, emotions, thoughts, or other behaviors that influenced my habit(s) today: _____
_____
_____

Daily habit check-in: Write in your habit(s) (such as "Sleep 8 hours") and check off those you stuck with today.

○ _____   ○ _____
○ _____   ○ _____
○ _____   ○ _____
○ _____   ○ _____
○ _____   ○ _____

DAILY CHECK-IN (DAY 40)

DATE: __/__/__

Today I'm grateful for: ....
....
....

Today's habit goal(s): ....
....
....

Habit motivation check:

☐ 1 (I really don't care.)
☐ 2 (This is going to be a challenge.)
☐ 3 (I'm not enthusiastic, but I can do it.)
☐ 4 (I'm feeling confident!)
☐ 5 (I'm excited!)

Mood *(circle one)*: 😃 🙂 😐 🙁 😫

Situations, people, emotions, thoughts, or other behaviors that influenced my habit(s) today: ....
....
....

Daily habit check-in: Write in your habit(s) (such as "Sleep 8 hours") and check off those you stuck with today.

○ .... ○ ....
○ .... ○ ....
○ .... ○ ....
○ .... ○ ....
○ .... ○ ....

DAILY CHECK-IN (DAY 41)

DATE: ___/___/___

Today I'm grateful for: ....
....
....

Today's habit goal(s): ....
....
....

Habit motivation check:

☐ 1 (I really don't care.)
☐ 2 (This is going to be a challenge.)
☐ 3 (I'm not enthusiastic, but I can do it.)
☐ 4 (I'm feeling confident!)
☐ 5 (I'm excited!)

Mood *(circle one)*: 😃 🙂 😐 🙁 😖

Situations, people, emotions, thoughts, or other behaviors that influenced my habit(s) today: ....
....
....

Daily habit check-in: Write in your habit(s) (such as "Sleep 8 hours") and check off those you stuck with today.

○ ....   ○ ....
○ ....   ○ ....
○ ....   ○ ....
○ ....   ○ ....
○ ....   ○ ....

DAILY CHECK-IN

DAY 42

DATE: __ / __ / __

Today I'm grateful for: ....
....
....

Today's habit goal(s): ....
....
....

Habit motivation check:

☐ 1 (I really don't care.)
☐ 2 (This is going to be a challenge.)
☐ 3 (I'm not enthusiastic, but I can do it.)
☐ 4 (I'm feeling confident!)
☐ 5 (I'm excited!)

Mood *(circle one)*: 😃 🙂 😐 🙁 😩

Situations, people, emotions, thoughts, or other behaviors that influenced my habit(s) today: ....
....
....

Daily habit check-in: Write in your habit(s) (such as "Sleep 8 hours") and check off those you stuck with today.

○ .... ○ ....
○ .... ○ ....
○ .... ○ ....
○ .... ○ ....
○ .... ○ ....

84 THE EASY HABITS JOURNAL

WEEKLY CHECK-IN   **WEEK 6**

DATE: __/__/__

This week's habit goal(s): ....
....
....

What went well this week with my habit(s): ....
....
....

Where I struggled this week with my habit(s): ....
....
....

What thoughts, feelings, or situations influenced my habit(s) this week:
....
....

What I plan to modify for next week: ....
....
....

Advantages of sticking with my habit(s) this week: ....
....
....

Next week's habit goal(s): ....
....
....

> "Your little choices are going to become habits that affect the bigger decisions you make in life." —ELIZABETH GEORGE

DAILY CHECK-IN (DAY 43)

DATE: ___/___/___

Today I'm grateful for: ....
....
....

Today's habit goal(s): ....
....
....

Habit motivation check:

☐ 1 (I really don't care.)
☐ 2 (This is going to be a challenge.)
☐ 3 (I'm not enthusiastic, but I can do it.)
☐ 4 (I'm feeling confident!)
☐ 5 (I'm excited!)

Mood (circle one): 😃 🙂 😐 🙁 😣

Situations, people, emotions, thoughts, or other behaviors that influenced my habit(s) today: ....
....
....

Daily habit check-in: Write in your habit(s) (such as "Sleep 8 hours") and check off those you stuck with today.

○ .... ○ ....
○ .... ○ ....
○ .... ○ ....
○ .... ○ ....
○ .... ○ ....

DAILY CHECK-IN (DAY 44)

DATE: / /

Today I'm grateful for: ....
....
....

Today's habit goal(s): ....
....
....

Habit motivation check:

☐ 1 (I really don't care.)
☐ 2 (This is going to be a challenge.)
☐ 3 (I'm not enthusiastic, but I can do it.)
☐ 4 (I'm feeling confident!)
☐ 5 (I'm excited!)

Mood *(circle one)*: 😃 🙂 😐 🙁 �

Situations, people, emotions, thoughts, or other behaviors that influenced my habit(s) today: ....
....
....

Daily habit check-in: Write in your habit(s) (such as "Sleep 8 hours") and check off those you stuck with today.

○ .... ○ ....
○ .... ○ ....
○ .... ○ ....
○ .... ○ ....
○ .... ○ ....

UNDERSTAND AND TRACK YOUR HABITS

DAILY CHECK-IN (DAY 45)

DATE: __/__/__

Today I'm grateful for: ....
....
....

Today's habit goal(s): ....
....
....

Habit motivation check:

☐ 1 (I really don't care.)
☐ 2 (This is going to be a challenge.)
☐ 3 (I'm not enthusiastic, but I can do it.)
☐ 4 (I'm feeling confident!)
☐ 5 (I'm excited!)

Mood *(circle one)*: 😀 🙂 😐 🙁 😫

Situations, people, emotions, thoughts, or other behaviors that influenced my habit(s) today: ....
....
....

Daily habit check-in: Write in your habit(s) (such as "Sleep 8 hours") and check off those you stuck with today.

○ ....   ○ ....
○ ....   ○ ....
○ ....   ○ ....
○ ....   ○ ....
○ ....   ○ ....

DAILY CHECK-IN (DAY 46)

DATE: ___/___/___

Today I'm grateful for: ....
....
....

Today's habit goal(s): ....
....
....

Habit motivation check:

☐ 1 (I really don't care.)
☐ 2 (This is going to be a challenge.)
☐ 3 (I'm not enthusiastic, but I can do it.)
☐ 4 (I'm feeling confident!)
☐ 5 (I'm excited!)

Mood *(circle one)*: 😄 🙂 😐 🙁 😫

Situations, people, emotions, thoughts, or other behaviors that influenced my habit(s) today: ....
....
....

Daily habit check-in: Write in your habit(s) (such as "Sleep 8 hours") and check off those you stuck with today.

○ .... ○ ....
○ .... ○ ....
○ .... ○ ....
○ .... ○ ....
○ .... ○ ....

DAILY CHECK-IN

DAY 47

DATE: __ / __ / __

Today I'm grateful for: ....
....
....

Today's habit goal(s): ....
....
....

Habit motivation check:

☐ 1 (I really don't care.)
☐ 2 (This is going to be a challenge.)
☐ 3 (I'm not enthusiastic, but I can do it.)
☐ 4 (I'm feeling confident!)
☐ 5 (I'm excited!)

Mood *(circle one)*: 😃 🙂 😐 🙁 😫

Situations, people, emotions, thoughts, or other behaviors that influenced my habit(s) today: ....
....
....

Daily habit check-in: Write in your habit(s) (such as "Sleep 8 hours") and check off those you stuck with today.

○ .... ○ ....
○ .... ○ ....
○ .... ○ ....
○ .... ○ ....
○ .... ○ ....

THE EASY HABITS JOURNAL

DAILY CHECK-IN (DAY 48)

DATE: ___/___/___

Today I'm grateful for: ....
....
....

Today's habit goal(s): ....
....
....

Habit motivation check:

- ☐ 1 (I really don't care.)
- ☐ 2 (This is going to be a challenge.)
- ☐ 3 (I'm not enthusiastic, but I can do it.)
- ☐ 4 (I'm feeling confident!)
- ☐ 5 (I'm excited!)

Mood *(circle one)*: 😃 🙂 😐 🙁 😣

Situations, people, emotions, thoughts, or other behaviors that influenced my habit(s) today: ....
....
....

Daily habit check-in: Write in your habit(s) (such as "Sleep 8 hours") and check off those you stuck with today.

○ ....   ○ ....
○ ....   ○ ....
○ ....   ○ ....
○ ....   ○ ....
○ ....   ○ ....

UNDERSTAND AND TRACK YOUR HABITS

DAILY CHECK-IN

DAY 49

DATE: ___/___/___

Today I'm grateful for: ....
....
....

Today's habit goal(s): ....
....
....

Habit motivation check:

☐ 1 (I really don't care.)
☐ 2 (This is going to be a challenge.)
☐ 3 (I'm not enthusiastic, but I can do it.)
☐ 4 (I'm feeling confident!)
☐ 5 (I'm excited!)

Mood *(circle one)*: 😃 🙂 😐 🙁 😢

Situations, people, emotions, thoughts, or other behaviors that influenced my habit(s) today: ....
....
....

Daily habit check-in: Write in your habit(s) (such as "Sleep 8 hours") and check off those you stuck with today.

○ ....   ○ ....
○ ....   ○ ....
○ ....   ○ ....
○ ....   ○ ....
○ ....   ○ ....

WEEKLY CHECK-IN `WEEK 7`

DATE: __/ /__

This week's habit goal(s): ....

What went well this week with my habit(s): ....

Where I struggled this week with my habit(s): ....

What thoughts, feelings, or situations influenced my habit(s) this week: ....

What I plan to modify for next week: ....

Advantages of sticking with my habit(s) this week: ....

Next week's habit goal(s): ....

*Today, I am moving closer toward
my goals through my healthy habits.*

UNDERSTAND AND TRACK YOUR HABITS

DAILY CHECK-IN (DAY 50)

DATE: __/__/__

Today I'm grateful for: ....
....
....

Today's habit goal(s): ....
....
....

Habit motivation check:

☐ 1 (I really don't care.)
☐ 2 (This is going to be a challenge.)
☐ 3 (I'm not enthusiastic, but I can do it.)
☐ 4 (I'm feeling confident!)
☐ 5 (I'm excited!)

Mood *(circle one)*: 😃 🙂 😐 🙁 😣

Situations, people, emotions, thoughts, or other behaviors that influenced my habit(s) today: ....
....
....

Daily habit check-in: Write in your habit(s) (such as "Sleep 8 hours") and check off those you stuck with today.

○ ....   ○ ....
○ ....   ○ ....
○ ....   ○ ....
○ ....   ○ ....
○ ....   ○ ....

DAILY CHECK-IN (DAY 51)

DATE: ___/___/___

Today I'm grateful for: ....
....
....

Today's habit goal(s): ....
....
....

Habit motivation check:

☐ 1 (I really don't care.)
☐ 2 (This is going to be a challenge.)
☐ 3 (I'm not enthusiastic, but I can do it.)
☐ 4 (I'm feeling confident!)
☐ 5 (I'm excited!)

Mood *(circle one)*: 😃 🙂 😐 🙁 😫

Situations, people, emotions, thoughts, or other behaviors that influenced my habit(s) today: ....
....
....

Daily habit check-in: Write in your habit(s) (such as "Sleep 8 hours") and check off those you stuck with today.

○ .... ○ ....
○ .... ○ ....
○ .... ○ ....
○ .... ○ ....
○ .... ○ ....

DAILY CHECK-IN (DAY 52)

DATE: __/__/__

Today I'm grateful for: ....
....
....

Today's habit goal(s): ....
....
....

Habit motivation check:

☐ 1 (I really don't care.)
☐ 2 (This is going to be a challenge.)
☐ 3 (I'm not enthusiastic, but I can do it.)
☐ 4 (I'm feeling confident!)
☐ 5 (I'm excited!)

Mood *(circle one)*: 😃 🙂 😐 🙁 😫

Situations, people, emotions, thoughts, or other behaviors that influenced my habit(s) today: ....
....
....

Daily habit check-in: Write in your habit(s) (such as "Sleep 8 hours") and check off those you stuck with today.

○ .... ○ ....
○ .... ○ ....
○ .... ○ ....
○ .... ○ ....
○ .... ○ ....

DAILY CHECK-IN **DAY 53**

DATE: __/__/__

Today I'm grateful for: ....
....
....

Today's habit goal(s): ....
....
....

Habit motivation check:

☐ 1 (I really don't care.)
☐ 2 (This is going to be a challenge.)
☐ 3 (I'm not enthusiastic, but I can do it.)
☐ 4 (I'm feeling confident!)
☐ 5 (I'm excited!)

Mood (circle one): 😃 🙂 😐 🙁 😫

Situations, people, emotions, thoughts, or other behaviors that influenced my habit(s) today: ....
....
....

Daily habit check-in: Write in your habit(s) (such as "Sleep 8 hours") and check off those you stuck with today.

○ .... ○ ....
○ .... ○ ....
○ .... ○ ....
○ .... ○ ....
○ .... ○ ....

DAILY CHECK-IN (DAY 54)

DATE: __ / __ / __

Today I'm grateful for: ....
....
....

Today's habit goal(s): ....
....
....

Habit motivation check:

☐ 1 (I really don't care.)
☐ 2 (This is going to be a challenge.)
☐ 3 (I'm not enthusiastic, but I can do it.)
☐ 4 (I'm feeling confident!)
☐ 5 (I'm excited!)

Mood *(circle one)*: 😃 🙂 😐 🙁 😢

Situations, people, emotions, thoughts, or other behaviors that influenced my habit(s) today: ....
....
....

Daily habit check-in: Write in your habit(s) (such as "Sleep 8 hours") and check off those you stuck with today.

○ .... ○ ....
○ .... ○ ....
○ .... ○ ....
○ .... ○ ....
○ .... ○ ....

DAILY CHECK-IN (DAY 55)

DATE: __/ /__

Today I'm grateful for: ....
....
....

Today's habit goal(s): ....
....
....

Habit motivation check:

☐ 1 (I really don't care.)
☐ 2 (This is going to be a challenge.)
☐ 3 (I'm not enthusiastic, but I can do it.)
☐ 4 (I'm feeling confident!)
☐ 5 (I'm excited!)

Mood *(circle one):* 😀 🙂 😐 🙁 😣

Situations, people, emotions, thoughts, or other behaviors that influenced my habit(s) today: ....
....
....

Daily habit check-in: Write in your habit(s) (such as "Sleep 8 hours") and check off those you stuck with today.

○ .... ○ ....
○ .... ○ ....
○ .... ○ ....
○ .... ○ ....
○ .... ○ ....

UNDERSTAND AND TRACK YOUR HABITS

DAILY CHECK-IN

DAY 56

DATE: __ / __ / __

Today I'm grateful for: ....
....
....

Today's habit goal(s): ....
....
....

Habit motivation check:

☐ 1 (I really don't care.)
☐ 2 (This is going to be a challenge.)
☐ 3 (I'm not enthusiastic, but I can do it.)
☐ 4 (I'm feeling confident!)
☐ 5 (I'm excited!)

Mood *(circle one)*: 😀 🙂 😐 🙁 😣

Situations, people, emotions, thoughts, or other behaviors that influenced my habit(s) today: ....
....
....

Daily habit check-in: Write in your habit(s) (such as "Sleep 8 hours") and check off those you stuck with today.

○ ....   ○ ....
○ ....   ○ ....
○ ....   ○ ....
○ ....   ○ ....
○ ....   ○ ....

WEEKLY CHECK-IN `WEEK 8`

DATE: ___/___/___

This week's habit goal(s): ....
....
....

What went well this week with my habit(s): ....
....
....

Where I struggled this week with my habit(s): ....
....
....

What thoughts, feelings, or situations influenced my habit(s) this week:
....
....

What I plan to modify for next week: ....
....
....

Advantages of sticking with my habit(s) this week: ....
....
....

Next week's habit goal(s): ....
....
....

> I am in control of my attitude,
> my effort, and my behavior.

28-DAY CHECK-IN   DATE: __/__/__

My habit goal(s) for this 28-day period: ....
....

How often I was performing my habit(s) at the start of the last 28 days:
....

How often I am performing my habit(s) now: ....
....

I am making progress: ☐ Yes   ☐ No   ☐ It's complicated: ....
....

What went well with my habit(s) over the 28 days: ....
....
....

Where I struggled with my habit(s) over the 28 days: ....
....
....

What thoughts, feelings, or situations influenced my habit(s)
over the 28 days: ....
....

What I plan to modify for the next 28 days: ....
....
....

My habit goal(s) for the next 28 days: ....
....
....

I am releasing self-judgment
and embracing self-love.

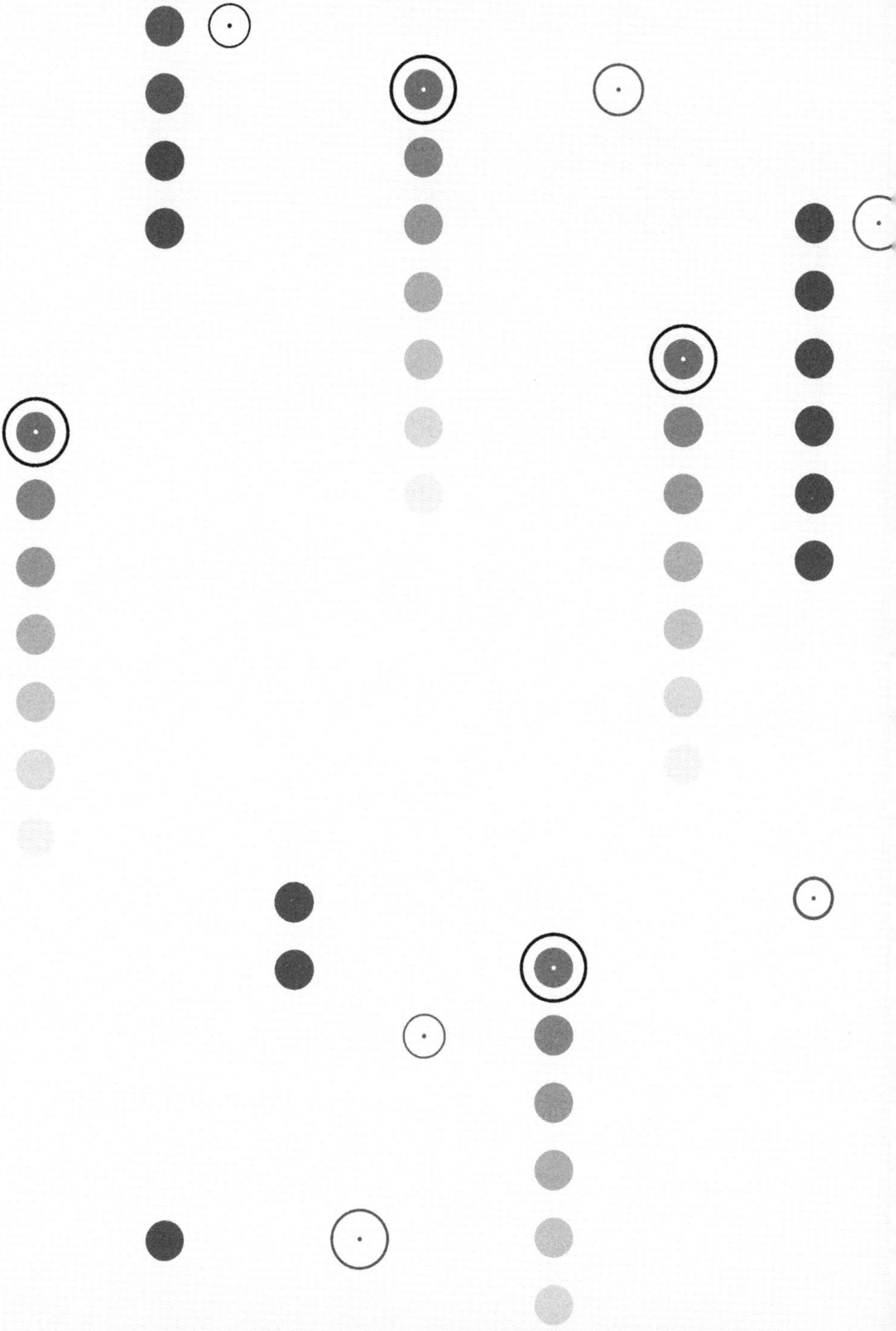

28-DAY HABIT CHART

Let's see how you went over the past 28 days. First, write down three of the key habits you tried to establish.

HABIT 1 ....

HABIT 2 ....

HABIT 3 ....

Then check which days you practiced them in the table.

	HABIT 1	HABIT 2	HABIT 3
DAY 1			
DAY 2			
DAY 3			
DAY 4			
DAY 5			
DAY 6			
DAY 7			
DAY 8			
DAY 9			
DAY 10			
DAY 11			
DAY 12			
DAY 13			
DAY 14			
DAY 15			
DAY 16			
DAY 17			
DAY 18			
DAY 19			
DAY 20			
DAY 21			
DAY 22			
DAY 23			
DAY 24			
DAY 25			
DAY 26			
DAY 27			
DAY 28			

THE EASY HABITS JOURNAL

28-DAY HABIT CHART

	HABIT 1	HABIT 2	HABIT 3
Completed streaks/days			
Goal streaks/days to complete			

Why I'm committed to these habits
How these habits reflect my goals and core values

....

....

....

....

Obstacles I might encounter   How I'll manage those obstacles

....

....

....

....

Notes about my habits that will be helpful for the next 28 days

....

....

....

....

> "Without ambition one starts nothing. Without work one finishes nothing. The prize will not be sent to you. You have to win it." —**RALPH WALDO EMERSON**

DAILY CHECK-IN (DAY 57)

DATE: __ / __ / __

Today I'm grateful for: ....
....
....

Today's habit goal(s): ....
....
....

Habit motivation check:

☐ 1 (I really don't care.)
☐ 2 (This is going to be a challenge.)
☐ 3 (I'm not enthusiastic, but I can do it.)
☐ 4 (I'm feeling confident!)
☐ 5 (I'm excited!)

Mood *(circle one)*: 😃 🙂 😐 🙁 😣

Situations, people, emotions, thoughts, or other behaviors that influenced my habit(s) today: ....
....
....

Daily habit check-in: Write in your habit(s) (such as "Sleep 8 hours") and check off those you stuck with today.

○ .... ○ ....
○ .... ○ ....
○ .... ○ ....
○ .... ○ ....
○ .... ○ ....

DAILY CHECK-IN (DAY 58)

DATE: ___/___/___

Today I'm grateful for: ....
....
....

Today's habit goal(s): ....
....
....

Habit motivation check:

☐ 1 (I really don't care.)
☐ 2 (This is going to be a challenge.)
☐ 3 (I'm not enthusiastic, but I can do it.)
☐ 4 (I'm feeling confident!)
☐ 5 (I'm excited!)

Mood *(circle one)*: 😃 🙂 😐 🙁 😫

Situations, people, emotions, thoughts, or other behaviors that influenced my habit(s) today: ....
....
....

Daily habit check-in: Write in your habit(s) (such as "Sleep 8 hours") and check off those you stuck with today.

○ .... ○ ....
○ .... ○ ....
○ .... ○ ....
○ .... ○ ....
○ .... ○ ....

DAILY CHECK-IN (DAY 59)

DATE: __/__/__

Today I'm grateful for: ....
....
....

Today's habit goal(s): ....
....
....

Habit motivation check:

☐ 1 (I really don't care.)
☐ 2 (This is going to be a challenge.)
☐ 3 (I'm not enthusiastic, but I can do it.)
☐ 4 (I'm feeling confident!)
☐ 5 (I'm excited!)

Mood *(circle one)*: 😀 🙂 😐 🙁 😫

Situations, people, emotions, thoughts, or other behaviors that influenced my habit(s) today: ....
....
....

Daily habit check-in: Write in your habit(s) (such as "Sleep 8 hours") and check off those you stuck with today.

○ .... ○ ....
○ .... ○ ....
○ .... ○ ....
○ .... ○ ....
○ .... ○ ....

DAILY CHECK-IN · DAY 60

DATE: ___/___/___

Today I'm grateful for: ....
....
....

Today's habit goal(s): ....
....
....

Habit motivation check:

☐ 1 (I really don't care.)
☐ 2 (This is going to be a challenge.)
☐ 3 (I'm not enthusiastic, but I can do it.)
☐ 4 (I'm feeling confident!)
☐ 5 (I'm excited!)

Mood *(circle one)*: 😃 🙂 😐 🙁 😫

Situations, people, emotions, thoughts, or other behaviors that influenced my habit(s) today: ....
....
....

Daily habit check-in: Write in your habit(s) (such as "Sleep 8 hours") and check off those you stuck with today.

○ ....   ○ ....
○ ....   ○ ....
○ ....   ○ ....
○ ....   ○ ....
○ ....   ○ ....

UNDERSTAND AND TRACK YOUR HABITS

DAILY CHECK-IN (DAY 61)

DATE: / /

Today I'm grateful for: ....
....
....

Today's habit goal(s): ....
....
....

Habit motivation check:

☐ 1 (I really don't care.)
☐ 2 (This is going to be a challenge.)
☐ 3 (I'm not enthusiastic, but I can do it.)
☐ 4 (I'm feeling confident!)
☐ 5 (I'm excited!)

Mood *(circle one)*: 😃 🙂 😐 🙁 😣

Situations, people, emotions, thoughts, or other behaviors that influenced my habit(s) today: ....
....
....

Daily habit check-in: Write in your habit(s) (such as "Sleep 8 hours") and check off those you stuck with today.

○ .... ○ ....
○ .... ○ ....
○ .... ○ ....
○ .... ○ ....
○ .... ○ ....

DAILY CHECK-IN (DAY 62)

DATE: __ / __ / __

Today I'm grateful for: ....
....
....

Today's habit goal(s): ....
....
....

Habit motivation check:

- ☐ 1 (I really don't care.)
- ☐ 2 (This is going to be a challenge.)
- ☐ 3 (I'm not enthusiastic, but I can do it.)
- ☐ 4 (I'm feeling confident!)
- ☐ 5 (I'm excited!)

Mood *(circle one)*: 😃 🙂 😐 🙁 😞

Situations, people, emotions, thoughts, or other behaviors that influenced my habit(s) today: ....
....
....

Daily habit check-in: Write in your habit(s) (such as "Sleep 8 hours") and check off those you stuck with today.

○ .... ○ ....
○ .... ○ ....
○ .... ○ ....
○ .... ○ ....
○ .... ○ ....

DAILY CHECK-IN (DAY 63)

DATE: / /

Today I'm grateful for: ....
....
....

Today's habit goal(s): ....
....
....

Habit motivation check:

☐ 1 (I really don't care.)
☐ 2 (This is going to be a challenge.)
☐ 3 (I'm not enthusiastic, but I can do it.)
☐ 4 (I'm feeling confident!)
☐ 5 (I'm excited!)

Mood *(circle one)*: 😃 🙂 😐 🙁 😖

Situations, people, emotions, thoughts, or other behaviors that influenced my habit(s) today: ....
....
....

Daily habit check-in: Write in your habit(s) (such as "Sleep 8 hours") and check off those you stuck with today.

○ .... ○ ....
○ .... ○ ....
○ .... ○ ....
○ .... ○ ....
○ .... ○ ....

112 THE EASY HABITS JOURNAL

WEEKLY CHECK-IN `WEEK 9`

DATE: ___/___/___

This week's habit goal(s): ....
....
....

What went well this week with my habit(s): ....
....
....

Where I struggled this week with my habit(s): ....
....
....

What thoughts, feelings, or situations influenced my habit(s) this week:
....
....

What I plan to modify for next week: ....
....
....

Advantages of sticking with my habit(s) this week: ....
....
....

Next week's habit goal(s): ....
....
....

I am confident I can achieve my goal.

DAILY CHECK-IN (DAY 64)

DATE: ___/___/___

Today I'm grateful for: ....
....
....

Today's habit goal(s): ....
....
....

Habit motivation check:

☐ 1 (I really don't care.)
☐ 2 (This is going to be a challenge.)
☐ 3 (I'm not enthusiastic, but I can do it.)
☐ 4 (I'm feeling confident!)
☐ 5 (I'm excited!)

Mood *(circle one)*: 😀 🙂 😐 🙁 😢

Situations, people, emotions, thoughts, or other behaviors that influenced my habit(s) today: ....
....
....

Daily habit check-in: Write in your habit(s) (such as "Sleep 8 hours") and check off those you stuck with today.

○ ....   ○ ....
○ ....   ○ ....
○ ....   ○ ....
○ ....   ○ ....
○ ....   ○ ....

DAILY CHECK-IN (DAY 65)

DATE: __ / __ / __

Today I'm grateful for: ....
....
....

Today's habit goal(s): ....
....
....

Habit motivation check:

☐ 1 (I really don't care.)
☐ 2 (This is going to be a challenge.)
☐ 3 (I'm not enthusiastic, but I can do it.)
☐ 4 (I'm feeling confident!)
☐ 5 (I'm excited!)

Mood *(circle one):* 😃 🙂 😐 🙁 😫

Situations, people, emotions, thoughts, or other behaviors that influenced my habit(s) today: ....
....
....

Daily habit check-in: Write in your habit(s) (such as "Sleep 8 hours") and check off those you stuck with today.

○ ....   ○ ....
○ ....   ○ ....
○ ....   ○ ....
○ ....   ○ ....
○ ....   ○ ....

UNDERSTAND AND TRACK YOUR HABITS

DAILY CHECK-IN (DAY 66)

DATE: __/__/__

Today I'm grateful for: ....
....
....

Today's habit goal(s): ....
....
....

Habit motivation check:

☐ 1 (I really don't care.)
☐ 2 (This is going to be a challenge.)
☐ 3 (I'm not enthusiastic, but I can do it.)
☐ 4 (I'm feeling confident!)
☐ 5 (I'm excited!)

Mood *(circle one)*: 😃 🙂 😐 🙁 😣

Situations, people, emotions, thoughts, or other behaviors that influenced my habit(s) today: ....
....
....

Daily habit check-in: Write in your habit(s) (such as "Sleep 8 hours") and check off those you stuck with today.

○ .... ○ ....
○ .... ○ ....
○ .... ○ ....
○ .... ○ ....
○ .... ○ ....

DAILY CHECK-IN (DAY 67)

DATE: ___/___/___

Today I'm grateful for: ....
....
....

Today's habit goal(s): ....
....
....

Habit motivation check:

☐ 1 (I really don't care.)
☐ 2 (This is going to be a challenge.)
☐ 3 (I'm not enthusiastic, but I can do it.)
☐ 4 (I'm feeling confident!)
☐ 5 (I'm excited!)

Mood *(circle one)*: 😃 🙂 😐 🙁 😣

Situations, people, emotions, thoughts, or other behaviors that influenced my habit(s) today: ....
....
....

Daily habit check-in: Write in your habit(s) (such as "Sleep 8 hours") and check off those you stuck with today.

○ ....   ○ ....
○ ....   ○ ....
○ ....   ○ ....
○ ....   ○ ....
○ ....   ○ ....

UNDERSTAND AND TRACK YOUR HABITS

DAILY CHECK-IN (DAY 68)

DATE: ___/___/___

Today I'm grateful for: ....
....
....

Today's habit goal(s): ....
....
....

Habit motivation check:

☐ 1 (I really don't care.)
☐ 2 (This is going to be a challenge.)
☐ 3 (I'm not enthusiastic, but I can do it.)
☐ 4 (I'm feeling confident!)
☐ 5 (I'm excited!)

Mood *(circle one)*: 😃 🙂 😐 🙁 😖

Situations, people, emotions, thoughts, or other behaviors that influenced my habit(s) today: ....
....
....

Daily habit check-in: Write in your habit(s) (such as "Sleep 8 hours") and check off those you stuck with today.

○ .... ○ ....
○ .... ○ ....
○ .... ○ ....
○ .... ○ ....
○ .... ○ ....

DAILY CHECK-IN (DAY 69)

DATE: ___/___/___

Today I'm grateful for: ....
....
....

Today's habit goal(s): ....
....
....

Habit motivation check:

- [ ] 1 (I really don't care.)
- [ ] 2 (This is going to be a challenge.)
- [ ] 3 (I'm not enthusiastic, but I can do it.)
- [ ] 4 (I'm feeling confident!)
- [ ] 5 (I'm excited!)

Mood (circle one): 😃 🙂 😐 🙁 😣

Situations, people, emotions, thoughts, or other behaviors that influenced my habit(s) today: ....
....
....

Daily habit check-in: Write in your habit(s) (such as "Sleep 8 hours") and check off those you stuck with today.

- ○ ....   ○ ....
- ○ ....   ○ ....
- ○ ....   ○ ....
- ○ ....   ○ ....
- ○ ....   ○ ....

DAILY CHECK-IN (DAY 70)

DATE: ___/___/___

Today I'm grateful for: ....
....
....

Today's habit goal(s): ....
....
....

Habit motivation check:

☐ 1 (I really don't care.)
☐ 2 (This is going to be a challenge.)
☐ 3 (I'm not enthusiastic, but I can do it.)
☐ 4 (I'm feeling confident!)
☐ 5 (I'm excited!)

Mood *(circle one)*: 😃 🙂 😐 🙁 😣

Situations, people, emotions, thoughts, or other behaviors that influenced my habit(s) today: ....
....
....

Daily habit check-in: Write in your habit(s) (such as "Sleep 8 hours") and check off those you stuck with today.

○ ....   ○ ....
○ ....   ○ ....
○ ....   ○ ....
○ ....   ○ ....
○ ....   ○ ....

120 THE EASY HABITS JOURNAL

WEEKLY CHECK-IN `WEEK 10`

DATE: ...../...../.....

This week's habit goal(s): ....

....

What went well this week with my habit(s): ....

....

Where I struggled this week with my habit(s): ....

....

What thoughts, feelings, or situations influenced my habit(s) this week:

....

What I plan to modify for next week: ....

....

Advantages of sticking with my habit(s) this week: ....

....

Next week's habit goal(s): ....

....

I am stronger than my excuses.

DAILY CHECK-IN · DAY 71

DATE: ___/___/___

Today I'm grateful for: ....
....
....

Today's habit goal(s): ....
....
....

Habit motivation check:

☐ 1 (I really don't care.)
☐ 2 (This is going to be a challenge.)
☐ 3 (I'm not enthusiastic, but I can do it.)
☐ 4 (I'm feeling confident!)
☐ 5 (I'm excited!)

Mood *(circle one)*: 😀 🙂 😐 🙁 😫

Situations, people, emotions, thoughts, or other behaviors that influenced my habit(s) today: ....
....
....

Daily habit check-in: Write in your habit(s) (such as "Sleep 8 hours") and check off those you stuck with today.

○ .... ○ ....
○ .... ○ ....
○ .... ○ ....
○ .... ○ ....
○ .... ○ ....

DAILY CHECK-IN (DAY 72)

DATE: ___/___/___

Today I'm grateful for: ....
....
....

Today's habit goal(s): ....
....
....

Habit motivation check:

- [ ] 1 (I really don't care.)
- [ ] 2 (This is going to be a challenge.)
- [ ] 3 (I'm not enthusiastic, but I can do it.)
- [ ] 4 (I'm feeling confident!)
- [ ] 5 (I'm excited!)

Mood *(circle one)*: 😃 🙂 😐 🙁 😩

Situations, people, emotions, thoughts, or other behaviors that influenced my habit(s) today: ....
....
....

Daily habit check-in: Write in your habit(s) (such as "Sleep 8 hours") and check off those you stuck with today.

- ○ .... ○ ....
- ○ .... ○ ....
- ○ .... ○ ....
- ○ .... ○ ....
- ○ .... ○ ....

UNDERSTAND AND TRACK YOUR HABITS

DAILY CHECK-IN DAY 73

DATE: / /

Today I'm grateful for: ....

....

....

Today's habit goal(s): ....

....

....

Habit motivation check:

- ☐ 1 (I really don't care.)
- ☐ 2 (This is going to be a challenge.)
- ☐ 3 (I'm not enthusiastic, but I can do it.)
- ☐ 4 (I'm feeling confident!)
- ☐ 5 (I'm excited!)

Mood *(circle one)*: 😃 🙂 😐 🙁 😨

Situations, people, emotions, thoughts, or other behaviors that influenced my habit(s) today: ....

....

....

Daily habit check-in: Write in your habit(s) (such as "Sleep 8 hours") and check off those you stuck with today.

- ○ .... ○ ....
- ○ .... ○ ....
- ○ .... ○ ....
- ○ .... ○ ....
- ○ .... ○ ....

DAILY CHECK-IN (DAY 74)

DATE: __ / __ / __

Today I'm grateful for: ....

Today's habit goal(s): ....

Habit motivation check:

☐ 1 (I really don't care.)
☐ 2 (This is going to be a challenge.)
☐ 3 (I'm not enthusiastic, but I can do it.)
☐ 4 (I'm feeling confident!)
☐ 5 (I'm excited!)

Mood *(circle one)*: 😀 🙂 😐 🙁 😫

Situations, people, emotions, thoughts, or other behaviors that influenced my habit(s) today: ....

Daily habit check-in: Write in your habit(s) (such as "Sleep 8 hours") and check off those you stuck with today.

○ .... ○ ....
○ .... ○ ....
○ .... ○ ....
○ .... ○ ....
○ .... ○ ....

DAILY CHECK-IN

DAY 75

DATE: __/__/__

Today I'm grateful for: ....
....
....

Today's habit goal(s): ....
....
....

Habit motivation check:

☐ 1 (I really don't care.)
☐ 2 (This is going to be a challenge.)
☐ 3 (I'm not enthusiastic, but I can do it.)
☐ 4 (I'm feeling confident!)
☐ 5 (I'm excited!)

Mood *(circle one)*: 😃 🙂 😐 🙁 😣

Situations, people, emotions, thoughts, or other behaviors that influenced my habit(s) today: ....
....
....

Daily habit check-in: Write in your habit(s) (such as "Sleep 8 hours") and check off those you stuck with today.

○ .... ○ ....
○ .... ○ ....
○ .... ○ ....
○ .... ○ ....
○ .... ○ ....

DAILY CHECK-IN — DAY 76

DATE: ___/___/___

Today I'm grateful for: _____

_____

_____

Today's habit goal(s): _____

_____

_____

Habit motivation check:

☐ 1 (I really don't care.)
☐ 2 (This is going to be a challenge.)
☐ 3 (I'm not enthusiastic, but I can do it.)
☐ 4 (I'm feeling confident!)
☐ 5 (I'm excited!)

Mood *(circle one)*: 😃 🙂 😐 🙁 😣

Situations, people, emotions, thoughts, or other behaviors that influenced my habit(s) today: _____

_____

_____

Daily habit check-in: Write in your habit(s) (such as "Sleep 8 hours") and check off those you stuck with today.

○ _____   ○ _____
○ _____   ○ _____
○ _____   ○ _____
○ _____   ○ _____
○ _____   ○ _____

DAILY CHECK-IN · DAY 77

DATE: __ / __ / __

Today I'm grateful for: ....
....
....

Today's habit goal(s): ....
....
....

Habit motivation check:

☐ 1 (I really don't care.)
☐ 2 (This is going to be a challenge.)
☐ 3 (I'm not enthusiastic, but I can do it.)
☐ 4 (I'm feeling confident!)
☐ 5 (I'm excited!)

Mood *(circle one)*: 😃 🙂 😐 🙁 😣

Situations, people, emotions, thoughts, or other behaviors that influenced my habit(s) today: ....
....
....

Daily habit check-in: Write in your habit(s) (such as "Sleep 8 hours") and check off those you stuck with today.

○ ....   ○ ....
○ ....   ○ ....
○ ....   ○ ....
○ ....   ○ ....
○ ....   ○ ....

THE EASY HABITS JOURNAL

WEEKLY CHECK-IN | WEEK 11

DATE: __ / __ / __

This week's habit goal(s): ....
....
....

What went well this week with my habit(s): ....
....
....

Where I struggled this week with my habit(s): ....
....
....

What thoughts, feelings, or situations influenced my habit(s) this week:
....

What I plan to modify for next week: ....
....
....

Advantages of sticking with my habit(s) this week: ....
....
....

Next week's habit goal(s): ....
....
....

> "If you always do what you've always done,
> you always get what you've always gotten." —JESSIE POTTER

UNDERSTAND AND TRACK YOUR HABITS

DAILY CHECK-IN (DAY 78)

DATE: __ / __ / __

Today I'm grateful for: ....
....
....

Today's habit goal(s): ....
....
....

Habit motivation check:

☐ 1 (I really don't care.)
☐ 2 (This is going to be a challenge.)
☐ 3 (I'm not enthusiastic, but I can do it.)
☐ 4 (I'm feeling confident!)
☐ 5 (I'm excited!)

Mood *(circle one)*: 😀 🙂 😐 🙁 😫

Situations, people, emotions, thoughts, or other behaviors that influenced my habit(s) today: ....
....
....

Daily habit check-in: Write in your habit(s) (such as "Sleep 8 hours") and check off those you stuck with today.

○ .... ○ ....
○ .... ○ ....
○ .... ○ ....
○ .... ○ ....
○ .... ○ ....

DAILY CHECK-IN (DAY 79)

DATE: ___/___/___

Today I'm grateful for: ....

....

....

Today's habit goal(s): ....

....

....

Habit motivation check:

☐ 1 (I really don't care.)
☐ 2 (This is going to be a challenge.)
☐ 3 (I'm not enthusiastic, but I can do it.)
☐ 4 (I'm feeling confident!)
☐ 5 (I'm excited!)

Mood *(circle one)*: 😀 🙂 😐 🙁 😣

Situations, people, emotions, thoughts, or other behaviors that influenced my habit(s) today: ....

....

Daily habit check-in: Write in your habit(s) (such as "Sleep 8 hours") and check off those you stuck with today.

○ .... ○ ....
○ .... ○ ....
○ .... ○ ....
○ .... ○ ....
○ .... ○ ....

DAILY CHECK-IN (DAY 80)

DATE: __/__/__

Today I'm grateful for: ....
....
....

Today's habit goal(s): ....
....
....

Habit motivation check:

- ☐ 1 (I really don't care.)
- ☐ 2 (This is going to be a challenge.)
- ☐ 3 (I'm not enthusiastic, but I can do it.)
- ☐ 4 (I'm feeling confident!)
- ☐ 5 (I'm excited!)

Mood *(circle one)*: 😃 🙂 😐 🙁 😣

Situations, people, emotions, thoughts, or other behaviors that influenced my habit(s) today: ....
....
....

Daily habit check-in: Write in your habit(s) (such as "Sleep 8 hours") and check off those you stuck with today.

- ○ .... ○ ....
- ○ .... ○ ....
- ○ .... ○ ....
- ○ .... ○ ....
- ○ .... ○ ....

DAILY CHECK-IN (DAY 81)

DATE: ___/___/___

Today I'm grateful for: ....
....
....

Today's habit goal(s): ....
....
....

Habit motivation check:

☐ 1 (I really don't care.)
☐ 2 (This is going to be a challenge.)
☐ 3 (I'm not enthusiastic, but I can do it.)
☐ 4 (I'm feeling confident!)
☐ 5 (I'm excited!)

Mood *(circle one)*: 😃 🙂 😐 🙁 😫

Situations, people, emotions, thoughts, or other behaviors that influenced my habit(s) today: ....
....
....

Daily habit check-in: Write in your habit(s) (such as "Sleep 8 hours") and check off those you stuck with today.

○ .... ○ ....
○ .... ○ ....
○ .... ○ ....
○ .... ○ ....
○ .... ○ ....

UNDERSTAND AND TRACK YOUR HABITS

DAILY CHECK-IN (DAY 82)

DATE: __/__/__

Today I'm grateful for: ....
....
....

Today's habit goal(s): ....
....
....

Habit motivation check:

☐ 1 (I really don't care.)
☐ 2 (This is going to be a challenge.)
☐ 3 (I'm not enthusiastic, but I can do it.)
☐ 4 (I'm feeling confident!)
☐ 5 (I'm excited!)

Mood *(circle one)*: 😄 🙂 😐 🙁 😣

Situations, people, emotions, thoughts, or other behaviors that influenced my habit(s) today: ....
....
....

Daily habit check-in: Write in your habit(s) (such as "Sleep 8 hours") and check off those you stuck with today.

○ .... ○ ....
○ .... ○ ....
○ .... ○ ....
○ .... ○ ....
○ .... ○ ....

DAILY CHECK-IN (DAY 83)

DATE: __ / __ / __

Today I'm grateful for: ....
....
....

Today's habit goal(s): ....
....
....

Habit motivation check:

☐ 1 (I really don't care.)
☐ 2 (This is going to be a challenge.)
☐ 3 (I'm not enthusiastic, but I can do it.)
☐ 4 (I'm feeling confident!)
☐ 5 (I'm excited!)

Mood *(circle one)*: 😀 🙂 😐 🙁 ☹️

Situations, people, emotions, thoughts, or other behaviors that influenced my habit(s) today: ....
....
....

Daily habit check-in: Write in your habit(s) (such as "Sleep 8 hours") and check off those you stuck with today.

○ .... ○ ....
○ .... ○ ....
○ .... ○ ....
○ .... ○ ....
○ .... ○ ....

DAILY CHECK-IN (DAY 84)

DATE: __ / __ / __

Today I'm grateful for: ....
....
....

Today's habit goal(s): ....
....
....

Habit motivation check:

☐ 1 (I really don't care.)
☐ 2 (This is going to be a challenge.)
☐ 3 (I'm not enthusiastic, but I can do it.)
☐ 4 (I'm feeling confident!)
☐ 5 (I'm excited!)

Mood *(circle one)*: 😃 🙂 😐 🙁 😫

Situations, people, emotions, thoughts, or other behaviors that influenced my habit(s) today: ....
....
....

Daily habit check-in: Write in your habit(s) (such as "Sleep 8 hours") and check off those you stuck with today.

○ .... ○ ....
○ .... ○ ....
○ .... ○ ....
○ .... ○ ....
○ .... ○ ....

WEEKLY CHECK-IN **WEEK 12**

DATE: ___/___/___

This week's habit goal(s): ....

What went well this week with my habit(s): ....

Where I struggled this week with my habit(s): ....

What thoughts, feelings, or situations influenced my habit(s) this week:

What I plan to modify for next week: ....

Advantages of sticking with my habit(s) this week: ....

Next week's habit goal(s): ....

I stick with things and don't give up easily.

28-DAY CHECK-IN   DATE: __/__/__

My habit goal(s) for this 28-day period: ....
....

How often I was performing my habit(s) at the start of the last 28 days:
....

How often I am performing my habit(s) now: ....
....

I am making progress: ☐ Yes ☐ No ☐ It's complicated: ....
....

What went well with my habit(s) over the 28 days: ....
....
....

Where I struggled with my habit(s) over the 28 days: ....
....
....

What thoughts, feelings, or situations influenced my habit(s)
over the 28 days: ....
....

What I plan to modify for the next 28 days: ....
....
....

My habit goal(s) for the next 28 days: ....
....
....

I am resilient, strong, and brave.

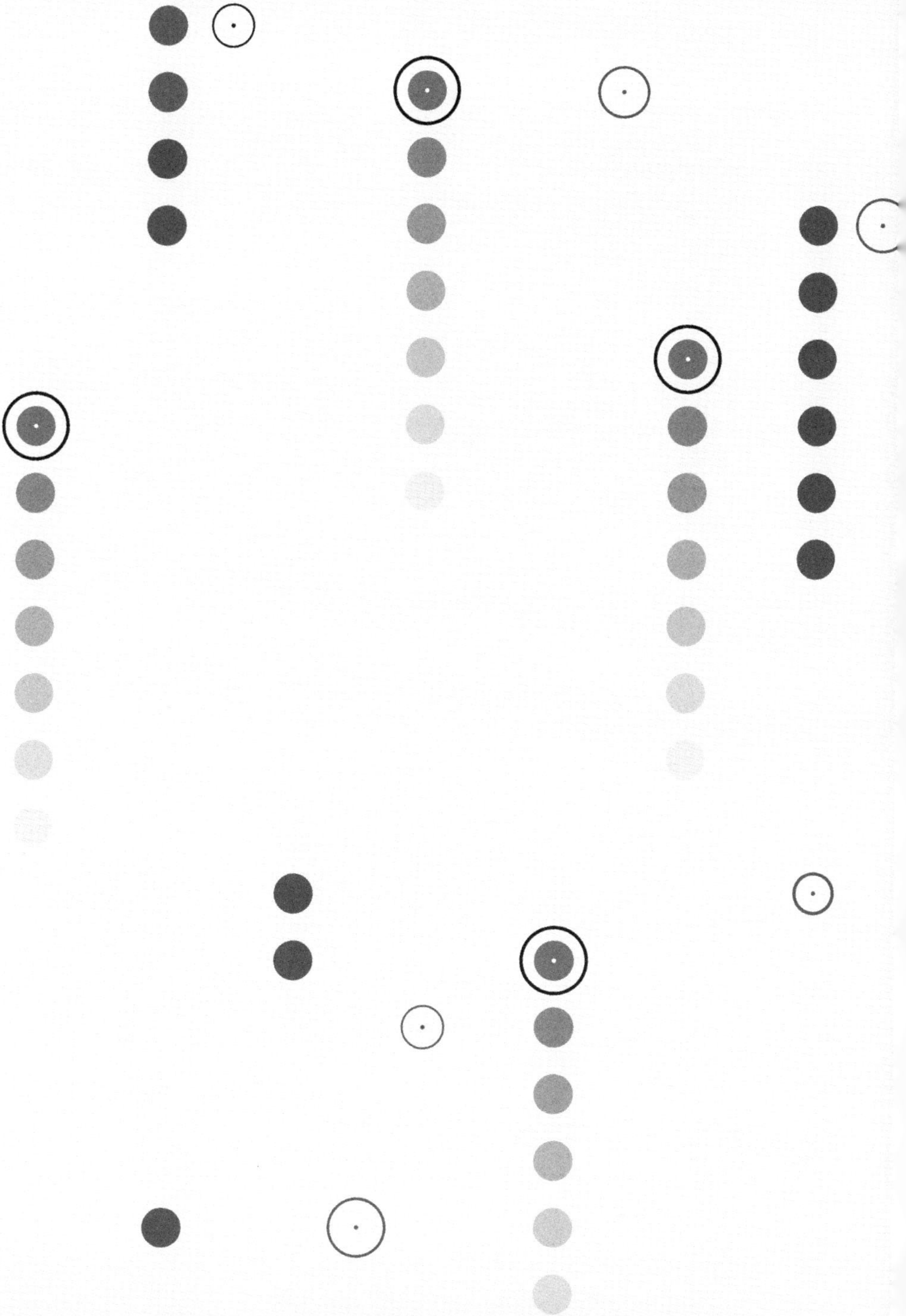

28-DAY HABIT CHART

Let's see how you went over the past 28 days. First, write down three of the key habits you tried to establish.

HABIT 1..................................

HABIT 2..................................

HABIT 3..................................

Then check which days you practiced them in the table.

	HABIT 1	HABIT 2	HABIT 3
DAY 1			
DAY 2			
DAY 3			
DAY 4			
DAY 5			
DAY 6			
DAY 7			
DAY 8			
DAY 9			
DAY 10			
DAY 11			
DAY 12			
DAY 13			
DAY 14			
DAY 15			
DAY 16			
DAY 17			
DAY 18			
DAY 19			
DAY 20			
DAY 21			
DAY 22			
DAY 23			
DAY 24			
DAY 25			
DAY 26			
DAY 27			
DAY 28			

28-DAY HABIT CHART

	HABIT 1	HABIT 2	HABIT 3
Completed streaks/days			
Goal streaks/days to complete			

Why I'm committed to these habits
How these habits reflect my goals and core values

....

....

....

....

Obstacles I encountered over the past 12 weeks	How I'll manage those obstacles in the future
....	....
....	....
....	....
....	....

Ways that I can monitor and maintain my habits in the long-term

....

....

....

....

> "It's only after you've stepped outside your comfort zone that you begin to change, grow, and transform."
> —ROY T. BENNETT

Final Note

Congratulations on making it this far in the journal! You started out on this journey by noticing a discrepancy between the life you were living and the life you want to live, and you recognized that your daily habits were contributing to that discrepancy. You were motivated to adopt healthier habits and ditch those habits that weren't serving you.

You soon discovered that habit change is a lot more complicated than we think. By tracking your habits, you've noticed that your motivation and effort don't necessarily result in consistency by themselves. But you've also equipped yourself with knowledge about the psychology behind habit formation. Changing habits isn't just about trying really hard—it's about uncovering the cues that drive the habit, adjusting your lifestyle to accommodate the habit, collecting data about what helps and what interferes with your habit, and consistently and repeatedly performing the behavior until it becomes a habit. You're now a scientist, running daily and weekly experiments to determine how to turn your goals into consistent daily habits.

Building new habits is definitely a challenge, but following the strategies in this journal will help you establish consistency. Be patient with yourself as you navigate the process—scientists' experiments rarely work as planned the first time around, and yours might not either. Use the results of your experiments to determine what to tweak tomorrow or next week. Build slowly and thoughtfully on your progress, taking small steps each day and each week toward your goal.

In addition to establishing the good habits that are an essential part of your self-care and living a valued life, hopefully you've made a habit of checking in with your journal every day. Keep going! Monitoring your behavior is one of the biggest ways to create change. You can do this.

Resources

BOOKS

Better Than Before: Mastering the Habits of Our Everyday Lives by Gretchen Rubin

Habits for Success: Inspired Ideas to Help You Soar by G. Brian Benson

The Power of Habit: Why We Do What We Do in Life and Business by Charles Duhigg

Tiny Habits: The Small Changes That Change Everything by B. J. Fogg

TED TALKS

Psychiatrist **Judson Brewer** explains how habits develop and introduces a simple but powerfully effective strategy to overcome addictive habits, like smoking and overeating. Watch at: Ted.com/talks/judson_brewer_a_simple_way_to_break_a_bad_habit.

Technologist and former Google employee **Matt Cutts** offers inspiration for setting and achieving goals. Watch at: Ted.com/talks/matt_cutts_try_something_new_for_30_days.

Social psychologist **Emily Balcetis** explains why some people have a legitimately harder time establishing an exercise habit than others. Watch at: Ted.com/talks/emily_balcetis_why_some_people_find_exercise_harder_than_others.

Psychologist and author **Guy Winch** explains why developing a habit of taking care of your emotional and mental health is critical for your overall health. Watch at: Ted.com/talks/guy_winch_why_we_all_need_to_practice_emotional_first_aid.

ONLINE SUPPORT GROUPS

Get Disciplined! is a Reddit community with advice and strategies to establish new habits. Join at: Reddit.com/r/getdisciplined.

Habits is a Reddit community for building, breaking, and changing habits. Members share strategies they have found successful. Join at: Reddit.com/r/Habits.

Develop Good Habits is a private Facebook group where members support each other in creating habits in their careers, community, finances, health, relationships, spiritual life, and beyond. They also offer accountability partners. Join at: Facebook.com/groups/182058985596545.

Happiness and Habits is a private Facebook group dedicated to habit change and accountability partnership. Its members also read books together to support continual personal growth and development around habit change. Join at: Facebook.com/groups/happinessandhabits.

APPS

Coach.me is an app that allows you to track your habits, and gives you access to the app's community where you can find support and ideas for sustaining your habit. You can also sign up for personalized coaching to develop or break your habit.

Done lets you track the habits you're building and the habits you're breaking. You can also use it to set reminders throughout the day to support the development of healthy habits (like drinking water or getting up from your desk).

Habitica turns setting habits into a game. As you reach your habit goals, you build up the stats for your avatar, allowing them to succeed in the game.

Loop is a habit tracker that will be helpful for anyone struggling with perfectionist tendencies. On this app, you develop a cumulative score that goes up for every day you stick to your habit, and drops when you slip up. For perfectionists, a day or two of slipping up can make it feel like you've ruined everything. But since your Loop score only goes down a bit when you slip up, it's a good reminder that all the progress you made still counts, even if you feel bad in the moment.

Morning Routine Habit Tracker helps you establish a healthy morning routine that will get your day off to a good start. It also minimizes how much thought you have to put into deciding what activity to do next.

Streaks allows you to set timers for time-based habits and will send you reminders when it detects that you're falling behind on your goals.

Strides is a simple habit tracker that allows you to check off your habits as you complete them each day, but it also lets you set flexible goals, such as streaks (e.g., three consecutive days) or averages (e.g., three times per week).

References

Graybiel, A. M. "Habits, Rituals, and the Evaluative Brain." *Annual Review of Neuroscience* 31 (2008): 359–87.

James, W. *The Principles of Psychology*. New York: Holt, 1890.

Patel, M. L., T. L. Brooks, and G. G. Bennett. "Consistent Self-Monitoring in a Commercial App-Based Intervention for Weight Loss: Results from a Randomized Trial." *Journal of Behavioral Medicine* 43, no. 3 (2020): 391–401.

Skinner, B. F. *The Behavior of Organisms*. New York: Appleton-Century-Crofts, 1938.

Wood, W., and D. Rünger. "Psychology of Habit." *Annual Review of Psychology* 67 (2015): 289–314.

Acknowledgments

Everyone needs an accountability partner for setting habits and reaching goals, and I'm fortunate to have six incredible ones—Drs. Marie Fang, Shawn Horn, Therese Mascardo, Sophie Mort, Diane Strachowski, and Zoe Shaw. You inspire me with your unparalleled accomplishments in making psychology and therapy more accessible. Thank you for encouraging me when imposter syndrome tries to interrupt progress, and thanks for making our mission to transform people a team sport—you epitomize women supporting women.

About the Author

Dr. Hayden Finch is a licensed clinical psychologist, behavior change expert, and dessert enthusiast originally hailing from coastal North Carolina. Duke- and Nebraska-educated, she is a go-getter with a passion for translating research into usable strategies, empowering others to be true to themselves, and dedicating herself to learning and personal growth. Her mission is to equip people with the skills to master anxiety, discover self-acceptance, and find meaning in a busy life.

Most recently, Dr. Finch wrote the book *The Psychology of Procrastination*, which uses psychological science to teach people evidence-based strategies to overcome procrastination. She also founded the Finch Center for High Functioning Anxiety, a clinic offering research-based therapy to help anxious and overwhelmed high achievers discover self-acceptance, confidence, and fulfillment.

Outside the therapy room, Dr. Finch is a waterslide enthusiast, a musical theater aficionado, and an ice cream connoisseur. For more information, visit HaydenFinch.com.